The Door Unlocked

An Astrological Insight Into Initiation

by

Dolores Ashcroft-Nowicki and Stephanie V. Norris

Published in 2009 by
The Wessex Astrologer Ltd
4A Woodside Road
Bournemouth
BH5 2AZ
England

www.wessexastrologer.com

ISBN 9781902405476

1st edition published under
ISBN 9781409270331

A catalogue record of this book is available at The British Library

The authors welcome feedback on this book. If you have a comment to
make, an insight to share, or a story to tell, please email us at:
author@thedoorunlocked.com
We cannot guarantee that every email will be answered, but all
will be noted.

The initiates who have shared their stories for this book have been
given pseudonyms and their birth data have been witheld for reasons of
confidentiality.

To

The One Great Initiator

ACKNOWLEDGMENTS

Stephanie wishes to thank:-

Dolores, who lent her name to this project from the very beginning, for waiting for me and for standing at my back all the way; all the people I interviewed, for their courage and openness in speaking to me and for trawling through their attics, garages and temples in order to find the answers to my questions; Anne Griffin, for her staunch support and encouragement, helpful comments and advice and for providing a Scottish eyrie in which to write much of this book; and all those others, both seen and unseen, who provided support of one kind or another on the journey that has been this book.

Dolores and Stephanie wish also to thank:-

Debbie Chapnick, for her beautiful artwork, painstaking drawing of the charts and for helping us to birth this book.

Contents

FOREWORD

There's a tradition in the Amazon Basin that no-one decides to become a shaman. Rather, you are called by the spirits, and if you ignore them, they will begin to persecute you. If you continue to ignore them, they are capable of making you ill or even killing you. Ruthless spirits. They know your destiny. They know you were meant to be a shaman. They will stop at nothing to ensure you achieve that end.

I've noticed the spiritual path nearer home is a little like that. You begin with a sneaking suspicion that there's more to life than another day, another dollar. You're drawn towards ideals and morals. You may or may not be conventionally religious, but you're certainly attracted to a spiritual life. Once you start thinking that way, there seems to be no going back. You might want the comfort of another day, another dollar, but it doesn't work any more. Something — your unconscious probably, although it may be God or spirits, I suppose — keeps saying, Waaaait a minute...!

It's worse if you make a formal commitment. It's much worse if you seek initiation.

Initiation is a word that's used more often than it's explained. You hear it bandied about esoteric circles like a New Year's Honours List or a promotion chart. But initiation is not the mystical equivalent of a knighthood or elevation to some post in senior management. It's a calling, a responsibility, a change in lifestyle and a royal pain in the ass. With initiation, you're right back in the Amazon Basin. Somebody up there, out there, in there, has heard your high-flown waffle and taken you at your word — no excuses, no parole. You picked the way of service and service is demanded. You made your bed, now you can lie on it.

Of course, nobody warns you. Nobody, that is, except Dolores Ashcroft-Nowicki and Stephanie V. Norris, although the terminology they use is much more ladylike than mine. For some reason, almost nothing has been written on the realities of initiation within the Western Esoteric Tradition since Dion Fortune penned her *Training and Work of an Initiate* in 1930. Even then, that work was largely concerned with historical provenance and broad principles.

How very different is the book you hold now. Here, for the first time I can remember, is something that tells you exactly how initiation is experienced through the extraordinary — yet extraordinarily obvious — approach of asking initiates themselves. It is also something that tells you exactly how initiation works through the equally obvious expedient of asking one of the premier occult initiators of our century.

And as if that was not enough, the hidden influences on the lives of initiates have been calculated astrologically through the technique of synastry and the relevant charts presented with full, detailed interpretations, to bring additional insights into the initiatory process.

All this makes for a fascinating document if you are a student of the Mysteries. But if you ever find yourself a potential candidate for initiation, then the book becomes less of an interest than a necessity.

It will remind you (if you need reminding) that...

- You must never, never, never take initiation lightly.
- There can be no genuine initiation without change.
- Initiation is not a reward, let alone a badge of office.
- Once initiation has been accepted, there is no turning back.
- As an initiate you are not a master, but a servant.
- Initiation is for life.

It will instruct you — fully and in detail — on one of the most mysterious and important processes in the Western Esoteric Tradition.

It will guide you through the most important spiritual event you are ever likely to experience.

Read it with the care it deserves.

Herbie Brennan
June 2008

INTRODUCTION

Initiation: Its Meaning, Effect and Promise

By Dolores

Initiate: *to begin; to be the first; to instruct; to let into secrets*
Initiation: *the process of initiating; formal introduction*

The above is the definition of a word that has intrigued the human mind since ancient times. It usually conjures up images of shaven-headed priests and chanting priestesses in Egyptian temples, misty with the smoke of incense and the excitement of unknown and long-forgotten rituals. These may include images of a trained neophyte undergoing tests of courage, endurance, trust and spiritual faith, but the idea of initiation always stirs the senses.

It was not just in ancient lands that these rites were enacted, we find them throughout history in many and varied instances. The act of priestly ordination, the enthroning of a pope, king or queen, the taking of the Hippocratic oath by new doctors, the christening of a child, the acceptance of a high degree from a university, right down to the rough and tumble endured by an apprentice when he/she finishes their required seven years of training. Though the last is seldom performed in our time.

Nevertheless such rites, rituals, acts of acceptance marked, and still mark the crossing of a threshold into a new stage of life. In occult terms it is a rebirth, the sloughing off of an old life and the taking on of new ways, new tasks and above all, new responsibilities.

Before we go on let me make a distinction between initiation and inauguration. The latter means to induct into a position of estate, which may be a lodge[1] or a special group. It is not an initiation, which pertains to the bestowing of a special grace or contact. In the occult one is initiated into an order or a school; one is inaugurated into a lodge or group within such a school or order.

Unfortunately initiation has become somewhat demeaned in our time. It is often handed out like sweets, demanding little or in some cases nothing of the candidate. Much is spoken of 'self-initiation' and while this is certainly possible it never holds quite the power of accepting it from the hands, heart and spirit of one qualified to offer it. Please note that I say offer...and not give, which implies the candidate has no option but to take; the candidate always has the option to refuse right up to the time when he/she comes before the initiator.

Initiation has also suffered from being used as a way of degrading the candidate, as in the often stupid and sometimes humiliating rites demanded before one can enter certain university and college groups. Some of these rites do have meaning and dignity, many do not.

It has been pointed out to me by a long-time friend that a lot of people regard initiation in the same way as they regard a medal. It becomes romanticised. Something to show off to their friends but they never think of the responsibilities such an event carried with it. Now I'm going to tell you the truth about initiation and you may not like it! There's nothing romantic about it, it is hard work, dedication and it lasts for life.

So what is the inner meaning of initiation and what makes it so important?

It represents an enclosing of the soul within the group mind of the school or order. Although they had the right physically to go in and out, they now *belong* spiritually in a way that is definitive. The mark of the order or that of the spiritual contact behind it has been placed in their aura.

But having been taken into the group mind, in another way they have been separated from the rest of the world. Initiation, at least in the First Degree, implies service, service to the order, to its Contact[2] and service to those in the outside world. You can only truly serve when you are an outsider, then you can observe from a distance and see what is needed. You must be able to distinguish between helping and letting mistakes be made in order to teach by experience. Initiation separates you from the group mind of humanity in order to serve it more efficiently. To sum up: the inner meaning of initiation is service, the importance is self-determination.

How does one become an initiate?
Why does it traditionally take three lives?

It may be hard to believe but initiation changes the chemical make-up of your body. People who do this kind of work and go through our kind of training have to be changed. Think of three days and nights lying in a stone sarcophagus as in the old Egyptian ritual, or the three years spent studying at a university. So why not three lives spent in coming to a point where you, your body, your brain and your mind are all ready for that one moment?

Hopefully one comes out of the process of initiation a changed person, a trained person who can leave their mark on the world and on the people they have met in their lifetime. Change is constant in this universe, we must all change all the time. But because the system of evolution and the mental and physical growth of any prime species are slow-moving and cosmic, the Lords of Light tend to look at their 'apprentices' through their bloodlines. They see a certain person getting interested and they steer them towards books, people and information. It might become a hobby. That may be your first life and as you get older you become 'marked', as someone who is to be watched over.

Those whose work it is to manage such things look around and say, Right, where can we incarnate this soul next? So they may place you in a family or a location where you will come into contact with like-minded people. But it will still be up to you whether or not you want to do it. There must always be free will. You may be born to a family where the emphasis on religion is so strict that you will eventually burst the bonds and look for something else. But this second life may have complications that will prevent you from doing anything more than maintaining a high level of interest in anything occult.

You might get to your later years before doing anything more than being interested. In the SOL[3] we have many people who tell us that they have been interested in spiritual things all their lives, but now the time feels right to do something about it. That can account for the second life. But by now the Lords of Light have you down as someone they want to train. It is at this point that free will becomes a moot point!

As the third life begins you are in the thick of it. They will move you around quite ruthlessly to achieve their aims. They would say, No, we are not ruthless, we are polishing you, you will become what we are now, you will take our place when we move on. It is now that you find yourself caught up in a vortex of synchronicity. Everything you have learned over the past two lives now comes together and you make rapid progress.

A school appears, you enter and find you 'know' the things you are being taught; you move ahead with ease and confidence. Then one day it happens and you find yourself standing before a closed door, a messenger beside you and trepidation in your heart. Initiation lies on the other side of the door.

What does it actually do to you?

Psychically it places the sigil of the school into your aura, physically it causes a reaction in the blood and the endocrine system. Think of it as a vaccine against 'flu, some people react to this with a slight temperature and a feeling of lethargy. Initiation injects something into your system that was not there before, so sometimes there's a slight response to this.

The 'seed' is placed in the top of the head, from there it moves down to the mid-brain, then to the early reptilian brain. From there it makes its way to the throat centre and finally it lodges, usually in the heart, but sometimes in the solar plexus. It can take a week or more to finally settle in place.

When it gets to the mid-brain it begins to affect the pituitary, often called the master gland. This is the moment when the reaction starts, usually 24/36 hours after the ceremony. There can be a sudden flood of adrenaline and you feel on top of the world and start looking round for dragons to slay! This is quickly followed by a slump and a feeling of exhaustion making you wonder if it was all worth it.

Before the initiation the cells of your body are...just cells. After the initiation every cell carries the imprint of the school's Contact. It can take a while for that to happen; in a few people it is almost instantaneous. With others the complete change can take longer, but mostly it takes about 12/18 months for every cell to become imprinted.

That's physically; mentally initiation jolts the glandular system and tends to sharpen the senses. You begin to notice the small things, to observe the world around with new eyes. For example, some time ago I was hurrying up a side street that has a reasonable amount of both car and pedestrian traffic. It has a very narrow pavement, no more than three feet wide. (I am writing this in Jersey in the Channel Islands and as we don't belong to the EU I can use feet and inches...) I looked down and saw, tucked into a minute space between the wall and the pavement, a single tiny flower. A brilliantly blue flower called a speedwell. Cars and people hurried past but no one saw it. The flower however couldn't have cared less, it was put there to flower and flower it did. When I stopped, I would be prepared to swear it was pleased. It made me feel blessed that one small flower had the courage to stand up and be counted. I blessed it and its nature spirit and went on my way. That is what initiates do, we observe, note, recognise and bless where it will be most needed.

Spiritually initiation prepares you for whatever your particular role or kind of service will be. It may well bring to the fore a talent you never knew you possessed. Later in the book we will look at what happens when, rarely, an initiation does not take, and at the differences between the First, Second and Third Degrees. Some schools offer many degrees, in the SOL we feel that three is more than enough. We do not even allot titles to our degrees, we let them speak for themselves. Simplicity is the key, elaboration diminishes the attention one needs to give to the candidate and the solemnity of the moment. So again: what is initiation?

It is a key with which the candidate can open the door to the world within, or they can look and decide to wait, and hope they will be given another chance. Sometimes the responsibility is so great they falter, close the door and return the key.

Initiation:
The Moment Of Rebirth

By Stephanie

It was the morning after the New Moon of 1 April 2003. I had gone to bed with the beginnings of a headache and now I awoke with my left temple throbbing and a dream vivid in my mind. In it Dolores had appeared and told me I was a candidate for initiation into the First Degree. This was not the first dream I had had about initiation: the previous May, the day after the Full Moon, I had started up out of sleep with a very strong feeling that 'it was time' I was initiated. I had been going to workshops run by Dolores for many years and had learned many things, but for some time now I had felt that I was on a plateau, which I was pacing restlessly, because I could not see how to get off it. The upshot was that I wrote to Dolores describing my dreams and we had a telephone conversation in which we set a date for my initiation.

Just under three months later, in January 2004 I picked up a copy of *The Guardian* newspaper to find a picture on the front page of a fashion model sporting a mask of Anubis, the Egyptian jackal god. Inside the paper the fashion designer, John Galliano's new collection, inspired by a recent visit to Egypt, was described as jaw-dropping. I was so struck by the picture that I rang Dolores up and asked her what the Opener[4] was doing on the front page of the newspapers. 'Gives a whole new meaning to the little black dress,' quipped Dolores, who has the Sun in quick-witted Gemini. It certainly gave a whole new meaning to something, I thought. Was the Opener indicating that it was now time to spread the word about initiation, which lies at the heart of the Mysteries[5], to a wider audience? In February I emailed Dolores to ask if she could recommend any books I could read on initiation. I got a reply straight back saying that she had never come across a book simply on initiation; after this she had put four exclamation marks. Then why don't we write one together, I thought.

The result is this book. I hope that you find it enlightening and that it will help you on your own path into the Light.

Synastry

In November 2004 I gave a talk at a SOL gathering in which I compared the birth charts of several initiates with charts I had calculated for the time at which they were initiated. This is an astrological exercise known as synastry, a word that is derived from the Greek for 'with' or 'together' and 'star'. The *Shorter Oxford English Dictionary*'s definition of 'synastry' reads: 'coincidence or agreement of the influences of the stars over the destinies of two persons'. I would add, or of a person and an event, such as initiation, for example.

Why should this be so significant? Because, as Dolores says in her introduction, spiritually an initiation is a rebirth. So a chart calculated for the start of the initiation ritual or the tying of the appropriate cord, where known, would give an astrological insight into the potential of the 'new life'. This can be clearly seen on a biwheel chart, with the initiate's natal planets on the inside and the planets for the initiation on the outside.

At any given moment the planets are in particular positions; a chart calculated for that moment captures or freezes it in time. The angles or aspects the planets make to the positions they were in when someone was born, or other key points in the birth chart, show how they affect that person or influence the course of their life. These are known as *transits*, because the planets are crossing or passing over these points and indeed may do so more than once according to whether they are moving forwards (direct) or backwards (retrograde).

In this book I look not only at the synastry between a number of candidates and their initiations, but also at what was going on in their lives, from an astrological point of view, in the run-up to initiation. Initiation begins at the moment you know you are going to be initiated, in whatever sense of 'know' that may be: a formal invitation, an intuition or a dream. In a sense an initiate's whole life, or lives prior to initiation, can be said to be a preparation for that moment.

I have picked out the main transits influencing their charts and followed them through: for example, in the case of Stephen, our male candidate for the First Degree, a Pluto opposition to his Sun; in the case of Erica, our female candidate for the Second Degree, a conjunction of Uranus to her South Node (see below) and Mercury. I don't go into exhaustive technical detail, because I don't wish those of you who may not know a great deal about astrology to be put off by terminology that may be unfamiliar to you (there is a glossary at the end of basic astrological terms used in this book). I would rather you went away with a sense of the insight that astrology can provide into your life, in particular of the light it can shed on the process of initiation, so as to enable you to maximise the potential of that moment.

You will notice that in all cases initiation or the build-up to it were characterised by transits to the Moon's Nodes, a prime indicator in the chart of the path or direction a person may take in life. I would like to say a word about them here because even among astrologers, particularly in the West, these key points in the chart are often overlooked.

The Moon's Nodes

The Moon has two nodes, North and South. In astronomy a node is simply one of two points where the orbit of a planet intersects the ecliptic, the name given to the apparent yearly path of the Sun round the Earth. You may find this easier to understand if you try to put one ring inside another, when you will see that they make contact with each other in two places.

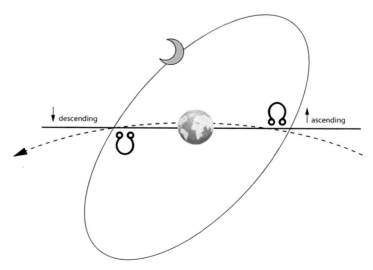

So the Moon's Nodes are not planets: they are the two points in space where the orbit of the Moon round the Earth crosses the ecliptic. Where the Moon ascends from below the ecliptic to above it, or from south to north, the intersection is called the North Node; where it descends from above the ecliptic to below it, or from north to south, it's called the South Node. The Moon's Nodes are always 180 degrees apart and retrograde; they take 18 months to transit one sign of the zodiac and approximately 18 ½ years to complete a cycle of the zodiac.

The symbol in the birth chart for the North Node of the Moon looks like a pair of earphones; the symbol for the South Node is the same, only upside down. They are always opposed to each other, so if the North Node is in Aries, the South Node will be in Libra; if the South Node is in the first house, the North Node will be in the seventh and so on.

The South Node is where we come from; the North Node is where we're going to. By sign, house, element and aspects to other planets, the South Node describes innate talents and abilities that we possess; something that we've done before or have experience of, such as relationships, parenting, material success or spiritual vocation. These we may have developed or acquired in a past life or lives. So we know this territory, it's second nature to us, we feel at home there – and in that lies the danger, because it's always easier to stay home than venture into the unknown. But that's precisely what the North Node requires us to do: to explore foreign territory, to develop qualities or gain experience that may be new to us and thus involve a struggle either with ourselves or with our environment. Hence the nodal axis' link with destiny, a word we don't always feel comfortable with in the West, because it seems to deny free will, by which we place so much store as individuals; whereas in the more collectivist societies of the East, there tends to be a greater acceptance of fate. In Vedic or Hindu astrology the Moon's Nodes are considered so important that they are given the status of shadow planets.

But it takes an effort of will to reach your North Node, as opposed to a blind acceptance of your destiny, whatever that may be; an awareness of the path to take in life. A planet conjunct or together with the North Node will help you to fulfil your destiny – as will someone with planets in the same sign. So if you have the North Node in Aries, for example, it helps to get to know people with the Sun or other planets in that sign, or in the element of Fire, because they have a quality that you are trying to develop. Conversely, if you have a planet conjunct your South Node, you may have a sense of continually being pulled back from the road to which you have set your face; or suffer from a kind of inner dissatisfaction that your life isn't all it could be. Which isn't to say that someone with planets in the same sign as your South Node won't help you to progress in life, but you may feel so comfortable with them that you're reluctant to make the effort to grow. In this book I also look at planets in square, or 90 degree, aspect to the Nodes, in the charts of those who have faced the challenges of initiation into the First, Second or Third Degrees of SOL.

The trick with the nodal axis is to integrate one end with the other: to use the qualities of the South Node to get over to the North Node. Very often this entails taking them up a level, which in turn involves letting go of old habits, old patterns of behaviour, old ways of relating – something we may not always be willing to do.

It seemed to me that this would apply particularly to initiates of a school such as SOL, called to serve to the highest level of which they are capable. In the following pages we look at how certain members of SOL chose to heed that call, the tests and pressures they had to face and the rewards of a life that, while sometimes lonely, fulfils the spirit in a way that a life lived solely in the material world may not. As you read, you may wish to ask yourself if you are ready to be called and if so, how you would wish to serve.

THE FIRST DEGREE
The Candidates

By Stephanie

"That leap, I think is what a First Degree initiation is – it's that leap across the unknown."

"Initiation is a catalyst... what it will do is highlight specially the weaknesses...it will develop the strengths, but it will face you with what you need to work on."

Know thyself.[6] The mantra of the initiate, or the person who seeks to voyage into the interior of the being, perhaps the most important journey any of us will ever undertake in our lifetime. This is where we start; this is what we must hold to when we step on to the path that leads to initiation; and this is what we shall return to time and again as we advance along it. For ultimately this is all we have, ourselves; not our houses, cars, bank accounts and all the other trappings of the material world, but the stuff of which we are made, our character, personal qualities, the values we hold most dear – loyalty, integrity, honour, love of friend, family or neighbour.

We all carry emotional baggage that we accumulate from childhood onwards and that on the path we will constantly be challenged to come to terms with, clear or jettison in order to be as pure a conduit as possible for higher or spiritual energy. The initiate best travels light, else his or her progress will be hampered, even blocked.

In these pages you will meet men and women who speak openly and honestly about their experiences on the way to First, Second and Third Degree initiation; the pressures they came under; the tests they had to face; and the difference initiation has made to their lives, on both the mundane and spiritual planes.

Their story begins with the family they were born into where religion or spirituality of one kind or another tended to be strong. Later at a certain serendipitous moment they picked up a book or performed a ritual or went to a workshop that set them on the path. Perhaps this will be such a book for you; we hope so, for that is why we have written it. Humanity is at a moment in time when it has never seemed more important for it to make a quantum leap in consciousness, to accelerate evolutionarily.

Monica: A Daughter of Eve

Our female candidate for the First Degree is Monica, an American woman in her 50s. Her father was a Baptist, her mother a Methodist, although neither practised the religion in which they were raised. They were a military family, constantly on the move and during her childhood Monica was exposed to several different denominations. In high school she became friends with a Catholic girl, who took her to Mass. "I'd never been in a Catholic church before…and I was kind of fascinated by all of this because I'd never really seen such ritual before…so I got talking to her about what's it all mean…but I felt drawn to it, I wasn't sure what it was that drew me – I don't know if it was the ritual itself, the candles, the community feeling – I felt a hunger that I felt could be satisfied there." The upshot was that Monica converted to Catholicism; she still 'once in a great while' goes to Mass but says, "in my own heart I've come to the conclusion that they are not the way and it bothers me, it saddens me that there are people who feel there is the way and that kind of imposition and requirement I think is dangerous and bad."

As a teenager, in college and beyond Monica read a lot of fantasy, occult and science fiction by some of the best-known authors of the genre, among them JRR Tolkien and Katherine Kurtz, whose work she 'devoured'. In *Lammas Night*, Kurtz' magical novel about the use of witchcraft, ritual and sacrifice in the defence of Britain during the Second World War, she came across Dolores' name. When *The Ritual Magic Workbook*, Dolores' classic work on practical training in ceremonial magic, came out in 1986, Monica bought a copy and worked her way through it. The internet came along, she typed in Dolores' name and found out she did tours.

It was in July 1998 that Monica met Dolores for the first time at a workshop she was running in Seattle, Washington. She picked up an application form for SOL there and 'thought and thought' about whether to join or not. Then three months later she went to another of Dolores' workshops in North Carolina and aired her doubts to her.

"I said, 'Y'know, I've kind of been here and there and hither and yon with this whole spirituality thing, jumped in with both feet over my head into Catholicism and now I feel that maybe I made a mistake with that, and I don't want to do that with this...I don't know – I don't know if this is what I need, I don't know if I have whatever it takes... Can you give me any advice, if I should try this or not?' Dolores looked me straight in the eyes and said, 'Well you've done it before – you can do it again. Trust yourself.'"

But Monica still wanted a sign that this was the right thing for her to do. At the Seattle workshop she'd been given a pot in which she had planted a seed. When she got home from the workshop in North Carolina it had produced a little flower. It was the sign Monica had been looking for. So she dried the flower and sent it to Dolores with her application.

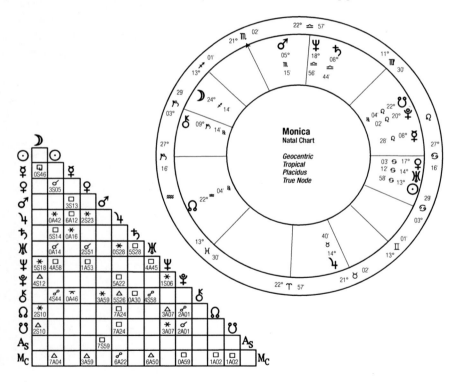

Fig 1

Let's now take a look at the astrology surrounding these two workshops, so pivotal to Monica's decision to take another spiritual path. Of major significance was the entry of Neptune into Aquarius in January 1998. It dipped briefly back into Capricorn in August, but on 12 October, two days after the workshop in North Carolina it stationed direct, to go forwards out of Capricorn and back into Aquarius in November. Since early 1996 this planet, associated with spirituality, mysticism and other worlds had been hovering around Monica's Ascendant in late Capricorn (*fig 1*); but now the mists had cleared, a guide had appeared and shown her the way.

Meanwhile Uranus, which had first entered Aquarius in April 1995, was one of several planets triggering Monica's natal Mercury in Leo, as the biwheel chart with Monica's planets on the inside and those for the October workshop on the outside shows (*fig 2*). On 20 October 1998, just over a week after the workshop, Uranus too stationed, in the same degree, a point it had been on and off since early 1997, challenging Monica to open up to new ways of thinking. On 1 July 1998, the month of the Seattle workshop, transiting Mercury had just entered Leo, only to go retrograde on 2 August, indicating it was time for a rethink. On 24 August Mercury stationed direct, only six degrees off her South Node, also in Leo. Monica was poised to move on in her life.

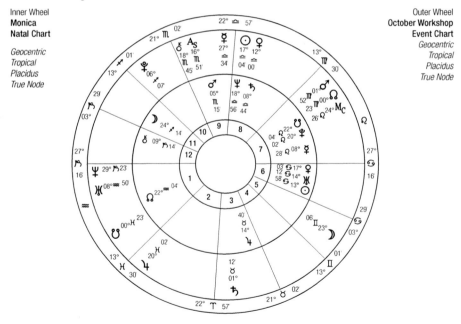

Fig 2

At the same time transiting Saturn was squaring her natal Mercury (as well as opposing her Mars), hence Monica's questioning of the path that was opening up before her and asking for a sign that it was the right one. Saturn likes to make sure of things and double-check the facts before it makes a move. But the helpful trine from Pluto to her Mercury pushed Monica on. Having made her decision, she was not to look back. We will take up her story again later in this chapter in the build-up to her First Degree initiation in September 2002.

But first let's meet our male candidate for the First Degree

Stephen: A Son of Adam

Stephen is a single man in his 40s. The guiding influence in his childhood was his maternal grandparents, who were both members of the Spiritualist Church. His grandfather used to travel round the country giving psychometric readings and talk about 'the other side' to him, 'so to me that was all quite normal and natural, really'. Like Monica, Stephen was an avid reader and from an early age read anything and everything to do with fairy tales and the supernatural. By the time he was five years old he had read *Grimm's Fairy Tales* from cover to cover.

He also used to 'speak to the trees', until he was told at school it was stupid and that there was no such language. He remembers climbing up a tree in his home village and sitting halfway up, in one of the crooks to meditate. 'I mean, I didn't know what I was doing at the time, but I'd sit up there, close my eyes and go off on an inner journey, guided by the tree.' With his Sun, Mercury and Venus all in Taurus, making a triangle of six planets in the Earth signs with Jupiter and Saturn in Capricorn and Pluto in Virgo, Stephen was born with an ease and affinity with nature and all her works *(fig 3)*.

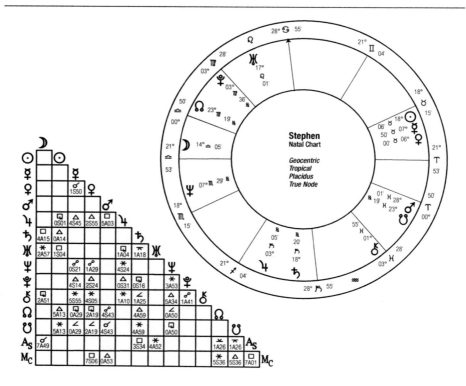

Fig 3

So how did he make the leap from all this to SOL? Once again it was a book that provided the bridge, a book that listed magical rituals that could be performed for each of the planets. The year was 1990, Stephen was 30 years of age and experiencing his first Saturn return, so called because this is when Saturn returns to its own place, by house, sign and degree in the birth chart. It's a major maturing life transit that happens to everyone as they come up to the watershed age of 30, an age when we are no longer in the first flush of youth and must seriously consider how we want to live the rest of our lives. In Stephen's natal chart Saturn is in the same degree as the Sun and only five degrees off his North Node in Virgo: he had reached a defining moment in his life, a moment that offered an opportunity to focus on the work of this incarnation. With Saturn also squaring his Moon and Ascendant the tension was building inside him to do something about it.

On 24 September 1990 Saturn stationed on Stephen's natal Saturn in the same degree, going forwards: the pressure to act was intense – it was now or never. Less than one month later Stephen performed a 'ceremony of self-awakening and increased sensitivity'. He did it to the letter – and within 10 days he'd met Dolores.

The date Stephen chose for his ritual was 18 October, the day of a New Moon in Libra, the sign of his natal Moon and also of his Ascendant. Mercury and Venus were also in this sociable Air sign, which is ruled by Venus, the planet that reaches out to others and makes connections. "I suppose for quite a while I'd been a solitary practitioner of magic and I remember thinking I needed to connect with like minds; I didn't know many, apart from my immediate family." As the biwheel chart with Stephen's planets on the inside and those for the New Moon on the outside shows, the planets in Libra all fell on or around his Ascendant: he could not have chosen a better moment to invoke other people into his life *(fig 4)*.

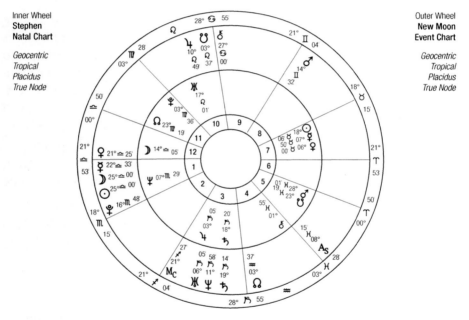

Fig 4

Stephen made careful preparations for what he called in his magical journal the Moon Spell. Everything is neatly and meticulously listed, from the layout of the altar and the lighting of a Venusian incense to the dedication to be reborn and guided to 'true wisdom and understanding'. The intent leaps off the page and intent, as anyone who works in this kind of way will tell you, is everything.

Shortly afterwards Stephen took himself off to town and found himself walking past a second-hand bookshop. "It's funny because I'd never walked past this bookshop before, but on this particular occasion I just felt drawn to it and I was looking in the window and I saw this very small flyer on Egyptian archetypes. I thought, I've got to go on that, I've really got to go on that."

The flyer advertised a workshop to be held locally the following week. "I walked in there and it was Dolores running the workshop. She said something like, 'Whatever you've done has worked' – 'What d'you mean?' She said, 'Well you wanted to meet people, didn't you,' so she picked up on something psychically straightaway. And she said, 'If you want to be connected, I'm a well-connected lady.'"

The Moon may have been the trigger – as the inner planets so often are – for the ritual that connected Stephen with Dolores and SOL but besides Saturn, there were other powerful planetary forces at work. Uranus and Neptune were also in Capricorn, opening up Stephen's Sun, Mercury and Venus in Taurus to an awareness of dimensions beyond the physical; while Pluto, in the first of three crucial oppositions from its own sign of Scorpio, was bearing inexorably down on his Sun. The stage was set for the rebirth that Stephen had requested in his Moon Spell: Pluto, Lord of the Underworld in Roman mythology (Greek Hades) rules transformation at the deepest level; in transit to the Sun it requires that you must in some sense die in order to rise anew.

By the time Pluto had moved on, in October 1991, Stephen would have experienced what he called 'an initiation by the gods' and his life would be forever changed.

The Judgment of Osiris

It was in April 1991 that Stephen went to another of Dolores' workshops, one of a series for those taking their first steps in ritual. The highlight of the weekend was a ritual called *The Judgment of Osiris*, one of Dolores' best-known which she wrote in 1987. At some point probably most students of SOL have taken part in this long and intense ritual, in which the heart of the dead king Osiris is weighed and he is judged by his fellow gods. He undergoes rigorous questioning by the 42 assessors, lords of karma, and must answer for the life he has lived. For the person playing the part of Osiris the experience is akin to an initiation.

But Stephen did not know any of this. To him "it was all just a big hoot really; we were all going to dress up like Egyptians and someone was going to be Osiris." "It's you," said Dolores, turning to him as she handed out the parts. "All right, OK," Stephen said, "that'll be a laugh."

Dolores took Stephen aside. She said, "This isn't something you can be flippant about, because if you're living a lie in any shape or form, you'll be found out." She told Stephen he could withdraw if he wanted to. This sobered him up but he decided to go through with it anyway. "I remember thinking at the time well, I do actually want to make sure I'm on my proper spiritual path."

The ritual was a profound experience for Stephen: he was trussed up like a mummy and put in a sarcophagus. Then he had to face the merciless questions of the assessors. He was completely honest in his answers. "I thought, I don't want the karmic fallout if I'm not – I mean, as soon as the ritual was coming upon me I was thinking, well actually I don't want to screw this up – I'm going to do this properly…and I'd done that earlier ritual, so obviously then I'd connected to SOL. I thought well, I've put myself in this position."

As Dolores had warned, Stephen's life changed completely: he became ill with meningitis; he split up with his then wife; he became homeless and had to live with friends; and he got a new job.

So what, I asked him, was the lie he had been living? "All sorts of things – I mean, sexuality was an issue, so not long after that I met my first male partner, long-term partner."

Pluto is ruthless in its destruction of the old for the new; it razes to the ground old outworn structures that stand in the way of the change that is necessary for growth. In this respect its action is rather like that of the phoenix, the mythical bird that burnt itself on a funeral pyre and then rose from the ashes anew.

For many years this powerful planet had been transiting Stephen's first and then second houses of self and personal resources, opposite the seventh and eighth of others and shared resources. In casting the Moon Spell at the time he did, Stephen in effect elected to put all these areas of his life up for change. Something of the sort is likely to have happened anyway: but far better to own the energy that have it come at you, to toss you about like flotsam at the mercy of a raging current. Stephen had taken control of his destiny and like Monica would not look back.

Years later he would be formally initiated into the First Degree, but for an impression of what it's like for the candidate completely new to initiation let's take up Monica's story again.

Emotions

Monica had in fact been due to be initiated into the First Degree in September 2001, but the events of 9/11 put paid to that. Dolores' flight was cancelled and Monica had to wait another year. By then she had already witnessed a First Degree initiation ritual, so the procedure didn't come as a surprise. But the emotions did.

> *"I really was the little lost barefoot bedraggled pilgrim asking for the way, knocking at the door of the Mysteries and the emotions just overwhelmed me – I almost couldn't speak the words. There was a desperation in me – that's the only word I can really use to describe it – I want in, I want to know in order to serve, I want to be on this path, I want – and there's just that, yes, let me in, ple-ase! Open the door!"*

Perhaps it was having to wait an extra year, but Monica was more than ready to receive the seed of light. "There is a part (in the ritual) where the star seed is dropped down, and then all of a sudden there was a sensation of yes! I don't know that I could describe it in any other way but an absolute yes! So that sensation of just total yes! made me feel that the initiation had taken."

I asked Monica how she had experienced the immediate aftermath of her initiation. She referred to a talk Dolores had given at a gathering of SOL lodges in November 2004, in which she had compared the First Degree initiation to a baptism.

Monica: I feel very much that it was that way for me; that the First Degree isn't so much about doing, or being, it's a *becoming*

SVN: a *becoming*

Monica: yeah...so there's a realisation... (*sighs*)...oh...y'know, I'm almost tempted to say that it's an acknowledgment that you're not crazy, that all this is true, and it's just that – I'm trying to remember a passage that's in a Gareth Knight[7] book about the inner tradition of the Arthurian legends[7], and he talks about initiation being a recognition that there are life and forms on other levels, and that initiation is just saying that this physical reality is not all there is to reality; an initiate is one who understands that that is so, who knows that this physical reality isn't all there is to reality; that there are forces and forms that we can't perceive with our physical senses, and that recognition is the First Degree initiation, and it can be an entire life's work getting to be able to harmonise with those forms and forces, work with those forms and forces, control those forms and forces. That First Degree is just the acknowledgment that you do understand that those forms and forces are there.

SVN: So it made you aware of them in other words?

Monica: No, I think what it did was it made me feel OK to be more aware of them.

SVN: So there was an increase in awareness?

Monica: Yes…yes.

This is evident from a look at the biwheel chart with Monica's planets on the inside and those for her First Degree initiation on the outside (*fig 5*). The Initiation Jupiter was on her natal Mercury, expanding her mental horizons; while the Initiation Neptune was opposing it, opening her up to an awareness of other worlds. It was important for Monica to 'feel OK' about this process because, as we have seen, her Ascendant is in Saturn-ruled Capricorn, perhaps the most sceptical and realistic of all the signs.

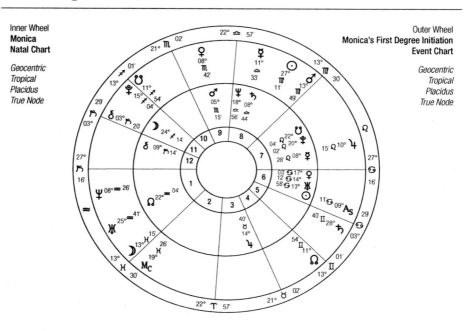

Fig 5

Monica was initiated into the First Degree the day before a Full Moon; the Initiation Moon was already in the sensitive, emotional sign of Pisces and less than one degree off her Sun in Cancer, which closely conjoins Uranus and Venus in this sister Water sign, ruled by the Moon. No wonder she could barely speak, so overcome was she by the tide of emotion rising with the waxing Moon, driving before it all rational thought and laying bare the naked desire to be borne over the threshold on which she stood into another dimension.

The Red Cord

By Dolores

The Initiator and the Source of Power

It is not only the candidate who has to prepare for the rite of initiation; the one who carries the Contact has to prepare the seed of light and lay down the path along which that seed will travel. The way is different for each initiator; there is no way of teaching someone *how to do it*. They must learn it from their own seed, received at their own initiation and then develop it slowly and carefully, growing in confidence and strength. To explain further I must go into more depth concerning those in whose names the initiation takes place.

There are many areas in which a Lord of Light may work. As a guide and mentor to those born to high position, most of whom are unaware of their unseen companions. The contact with the incoming king or queen occurs during the coronation rites of countries blessed with a monarchy. The bloodline, carefully monitored for many hundreds of years, will have had the same Lord of Light standing behind it. Where there is no ruler, but an elected or temporary leader, the mentor may change to suit the different incoming personality. This can also change the way in which the elected person is viewed by the populace.

A Lord of Light may choose to teach and so becomes the point of pressure behind Contacted schools and orders. The term 'point of pressure' is apt in that it is this pressure that keeps the order going for its destined time. His immediate task is to nurture each section of the school. Encouraging those who show promise and removing those who need to be in another place. Along with this comes the task of bringing in items of lost knowledge as and when the time is right for them to return. Other Lords of Light are given rule over entire countries, to guide them into ways that, often centuries hence, will enable them to come to full flower. All this is done with love, patience and compassion. As human beings the matter of our bodies is made up of particles of vibrating light. Not a truly accurate description, but one easily visualised. The vehicle of a Lord of Light is also made up of such particles, but of infinitely finer and purer vibrations plus – and this is the important part – each and every particle is a hologram. That is to say, one particle is also the whole Teacher. In this way a Lord of Light can touch, teach, instruct and nurture as many human beings as needed and give full attention to each one. But there are billions of particles in the light bodies of these Masters, more than are needed for that area of their work, so the particles not used are now available to become the seeds given at initiation.

The Seed of Light

When you receive your first initiation the seed of light is implanted and will take up its position in the head, heart or solar plexus. No one position is more important than another; it is just the point where a seed can access the higher self of the candidate most easily, via the energy, the emotions or the intellect. Sometimes it will move from area to area, or it may remain in one place; more rarely it can extend itself like dendrites in the brain and put out filaments that connect all three. The seed remains in the subtle body for life. At death it unites with the spiritual essence and departs with it under the guidance of the Lord of Light to whom one is bound.

When preparing to initiate a candidate the initiator must prepare the seed in themselves, for that is the source of power. One must think deeply about the rite and the candidate. The initiator must be certain that there is a spiritual conduit ready, one that can hold power. This is because the candidate at the moment of the passing of power becomes a chalice, emptied of self and ready to take in that which is being offered.

A few hours before the ritual, the initiator must concentrate on the seed within and feed it energy, love and power via the three Rays.[8] Thus filled, it will split into as many portions as will be needed, leaving the original to recuperate and regrow. The 'seedlings' now move from their starting point to the thymus gland where they rest until summoned.

The thymus gland is situated in the lower part of the neck and throat area. Although large in newborns and young children, it shrinks and becomes more or less inactive in adulthood making it virtually 'an empty compartment' where the seed(s) can wait until needed. It does not interfere with any vital workings of the body, but it is close to the pathway the seed must take, down the right arm and into the fingers where it is held just seconds prior to its insertion into the fontanelle of the candidate.

The Initiation

The actual ceremony does not take long; the most important moment is the implantation of the seed. The rite itself varies considerably from school to school and from order to order; some rites are more elaborate than others. Never judge a ritual by its length or the amount of 'dressing' that goes with it. Traditional pomp and circumstance can be wonderful at the right time and place, but initiations should be simple, straightforward and not too long. Too much elaboration means attention is taken away from (a) the candidate and (b) the actual meaning of the ritual.

The candidate should be kept away from people and given time to contemplate what lies ahead. A quiet area to sit and gather themselves together is needed. A picture of significance to the school or order is good to look at and to remind them of the aims of the school. In SOL they are robed, barefooted and carry with them a small silver coin.

When all is prepared a messenger is usually despatched to guide the candidate to the door. Here they may be questioned, so they should have their answers ready. When finally they knock at the door, they may be refused several times before being admitted and then only when blindfolded.

Once within sacred space they may have to submit to having their feet ceremoniously cleansed; in effect they have left the everyday world and are now in the realms of the spirit. They may now be subjected to more questions and/or a series of tests. They will almost certainly come before the main officers, who will ask for affirmations. If all goes well and they answer correctly, they will finally come before the initiator and the blindfold will be taken away. What follows differs from one school to another, but it culminates in a series of small events leading up to the actual implantation.

There will be a cleansing, a presentation to the Elements, a hallowing or censing and the head, hands and heart may be anointed. Now comes the actual initiation. *The thing to remember is that at this moment the officer in front of you is only a channel for what is coming through him or her.* Don't confuse the human being with what is focussing through them at that moment. Don't try to remember what words are spoken; words do not matter, it is what happens that is important.

You will feel pressure on your head, your forehead, your throat and your heart centre. The seed will be astrally, mentally and spiritually pushed down into your head. It may be guided further on its journey if the initiator has clear sight and already knows where it is destined to rest. Just relax and open yourself as much as you can. Let the moment guide you. You feel a little dizzy, but you won't fall; there are supporters all around you. At this moment in time YOU are the focus not only of those in the temple, but those on the subtle levels who have gathered to act as witnesses. This space is filled with love, power and compassion for one person: YOU.

After a few moments you will be presented with your new cord, usually a red one signifying that you are now an initiate of the First Degree and your magical ring will be placed on your finger, marrying you to the Mysteries. Finally you will be conducted to your seat in the temple. As you sit and look around, you will see smiling faces wishing you well. You now take your place among them, following an ancient tradition.

What does this ceremony mean?

Basically it means you have grown up in the spiritual sense. To wear the red cord means you have now opted to take full responsibility for all your actions. You may think you already do this. Not in the way it is meant within the Mysteries.

In every Age there comes to birth, sooner or later, the Christ Force of that Age. This is one of the highest-level Lords of Light. It might be one of the Lords of Form, or a Lord of Mind; if the need is great at the time it will be a Lord of Flame. It incarnates in human form, the equivalent of living in a stable among animals after having existed in a body of pure light. Yet such is the love and the power that the change is accepted freely.

The Saviours, the Christs, are always destined to die a sacrificial death. They are there to cause the turning point in that Age and to open the way to new wisdom and knowledge. The Age of Pisces was an age that came in on the ray of love. The Aquarian Age brings in an age of knowledge and the expansion of intellect.

Nothing is ever given free, not love, not power, not knowledge. We pay in part for the things we want: we pay for schooling, for health, for wisdom, for love; for everything we possess we have paid, not always in money but in time, effort, attention, etc. We pay for what we want, use and have during the span of our lives. *The Christ of the Age pays for all life on Earth, for the entire Age.* Pays continuously. I have heard people say, 'Christ came down from the cross, He is no longer nailed there.' But this is one area where the Catholic Church has it right. To them the crucifix is a constant reminder that the Christ is still carrying the weight and the pain and will do so until we learn to take responsibility for ourselves. The physical cross may have gone, but the spiritual cross still carries its burden.

So where does the work of the initiate come in? Did you think you came to this path for your own benefit? Think again. You are, as every initiate has been since the beginning, on this path for those who have yet to come out of the shadows. Yes, you come for yourself, but you also come for them.

Every pain, every sorrow, every tragedy, every rotten thing that happens, every tear, every moment of agony is shared by the Christ of the Age, on and on for the whole of the Age. Every lie, every deed of revenge and hatred, every murder, every betrayal adds to the weight, adds to the agony. Equally, every joy, every laugh, every moment of love, compassion, praise and hope will lift the weight and offer relief. The average human being does not know, understand or care. So the Christ accepts it all.

An initiate of the First Degree takes over from the Christ full responsibility for everything he or she does. That means for as long as they are in the First Degree, every action or deed incurs retribution that must be accepted. At this point in their training they may also take on some service in the form of training, supervising, etc. When you train someone in the work of the Mysteries you must also take some, though not all, of the responsibility for your students. You are their teacher; if you teach them wrongly you are to blame, not they. So being an initiate is not just a status thing, it is not a medal for good behaviour; it is a task, often a hard one.

Does being an initiate have anything good to offer?

Yes, it increases your ability to understand, to absorb teaching at a higher level and opens the heart centre to the extent that you are able to offer the power of the heart to those in need. It brings an inner joy into your life that comes from actually being of use both to a Lord of Light and to the Aeon of the Age. It increases the effectiveness of the five senses and increases your awareness of life around you.

What does the First Degree ask of the initiate?

In a word: service. You come to this degree presumably with a certain amount of training, understanding of your tradition and an ability to cope with its pressures. No school can stand alone for long. It needs the support of its students and initiates. No matter how dedicated its leaders, the students and teachers form its foundation. Unless that is strong it will not prevail.

Schools and orders are not infinite, they will come to an end in time. They do what they can and then seemingly die. Only we all know that is not true; death is merely a change. The Contact lies dormant until the right one comes along, then like a sleeping beauty it wakens to the kiss of love. If the work has been good, parts of the school will go on. Think of it as a family – mother, father and children. The children are the offshoots of the school; they grow up and leave home and establish their own families. The parents die but the bloodline goes on.

Does an initiation ever go wrong?

Yes, it can. It does not happen often, but it does. Then the responsibility falls on the physical plane teacher. It is their task to choose carefully and to know when someone is worthy of the red cord. But no matter how advanced a teacher, they are after all human and make mistakes. Even if the failed initiate acted deliberately to undermine the teacher or if an unexpected life event causes the failure, it still falls upon the teacher. That is their service!

There are many reasons why this happens:-

1. Simply because the person was not as ready as was thought and the pressure was too much;

2. It may cause a sudden opening up of psychic awareness that the person is totally unprepared for. This can cause problems that involve families and work and can break up marriages;

3. The person involved has a character flaw that has been well hidden and comes to the surface in the form of anger, resentment and desire for revenge;

4. A person may become seriously ill and unable to fulfil their tasks;

5. The initiate lies during the ritual.

Initiation once given cannot be taken back. It remains potent and in working order. A priest may turn out to be a liar, a cheat and worse, BUT when he says Mass *it is real and, importantly, pure*. This is a safeguard for those who have placed their trust in him. They must not be left untended, so whatever the priest may have done, what he DOES in the Mass is kept pure by the power of God who will not allow His/Her children to suffer because of one who has gone astray. A priest may be 'unfrocked' but he can still say Mass in private. Once an initiate, always an initiate; the door is never completely closed.

Occasionally someone will desire initiation for the purpose of acquiring power over others. They can be plausible, charming and seemingly open.

They are often quick to learn and knowledgable. Every Eden has its serpent. Once the dark seed is sown, the play must run its course. But the Lords of Light take the view that nothing is entirely bad and often They turn the whole scenario into a test for those who have been the unwitting cause of the event.

If the lesson is recognised, understood and learned from, for the initiator it can become a valuable tool for it can show you how strong you can be, if the need is great enough. Then comes the even greater test. If you can forgive what was done and be thankful for the test that made you realise your own strength, then a greater battle than you know has been won.

Every initiation is a test for both the candidate and the initiator; both are taking a risk, both are going on blind faith, both must trust each other. Better to wait a little longer and be sure, then burden someone with a spiritual weight that is too much for them to carry.

The Chosen Road

By Stephanie

"In the ritual it says, what is the requirement of the First Degree? (Answer) inner balance and harmony, and I think that does come in more strongly...there's just a calmer acceptance and harmony within."

"I've found a faith; there's a certain...like a bedrock of faith with me now; I know that I will be guided...I know I have the capabilities and wherewithal to do things, whereas before I might not have done it."

In the ritual for the SOL First Degree initiation the candidate is asked what he or she is doing 'on this lonely road'. The candidate replies, 'This is the road I have chosen to tread.' Hence the title of the third section of this chapter. But what are the consequences of travelling the chosen road, the way that has opened?

In Part One of this chapter we left Stephen dealing with the aftermath of his 'initiation by the gods' in April 1991; he was not formally initiated into the First Degree, which he refers to as his initiation by his teachers, until November 2004. Why, I wondered, was there such a long gap, nearly 14 years, between the two initiations? Stephen reminded me that just before he was initiated, his partner, James had died of cancer. Stephen didn't actually think he was going to be able to make it to his initiation, but James made him promise that he would go. "I said to James, 'No, I've already spent one weekend with SOL away from you; that's it now, so until you go I'll be with you every weekend.' And James said, 'No, I'm going before then – I know when I'm going, but I want you to promise me that you'll honour it and go through with your initiation.'"

James died almost three weeks to the day of Stephen's First Degree initiation, leaving him to experience all the complex emotions around the death of someone you love. In that sense James was his initiator and I would like to say here something that I have often thought: that the great watersheds of life – the birth of a child, marriage, the death of someone close to you – are as much initiations in their way as the spiritual initiation that this book is about. Of course, one may lead to the other as in Stephen's case. So pay attention to what happens in the run-up to initiation; it's an integral part of the initiation itself.

Which takes me back to where it all began, with Stephen playing the part of Osiris in *The Judgment of Osiris*. This was of course an experience of death on some level, if not the physical and we have seen how Stephen's life changed completely afterwards. You could say that having 'died', he was reborn and so is in a unique position to help others make that transition between life and death, as he did for James. This is the role of psychopomp, the guide of souls to their place of rest; one of the guises of Anubis, who passes between the worlds, this and the other, taking by the hand those whose time has come to make the journey, going before, opening the way. With his Moon in Libra tucked away in the 12th house, Stephen is a natural mediator between the seen and the unseen.

As I've already mentioned, the *Judgment of Osiris* and the Moon Spell that preceded it were characterised by a massive opposition of Pluto to Stephen's Sun. By the time of James's death and Stephen's First Degree initiation the planet of transformation had moved on to Sagittarius. In the chart for the initiation itself it occupies a dominant position: only 10 degrees off the Ascendant and ruling the Sun, Mars and South Node in Scorpio as well as the Midheaven (*fig 6*).

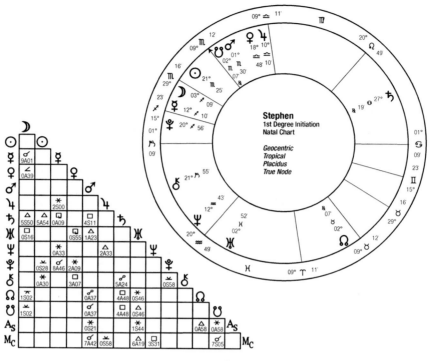

Fig 6

The biwheel with Stephen's planets on the inside and those for his First Degree initiation on the outside shows that at the same time Pluto was squaring his nodal axis together with Mars, which is conjunct the South Node (*fig 7*). Stephen's life was about to go in a radical new direction and James was to be the instrument of it.

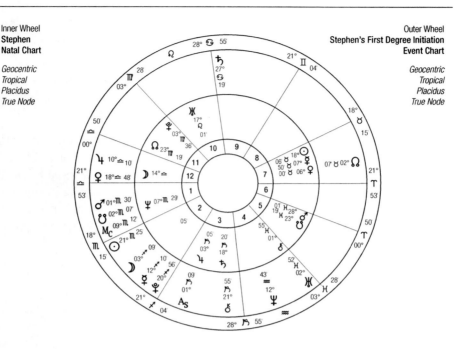

Fig 7

But first we must go back to January 2003, when Stephen had what he described as a profound experience on an introductory workshop on Neuro-Linguistic Programming (NLP). Incidentally this was run by another SOL initiate, Paul, whose story we shall take up in the next chapter on the Second Degree.

> *"When they did the emotional clearing and the timeline[9] stuff, it actually did clear something really major for me and that was like my fear of deep water, even though I wasn't working on that; it was because it was a generic clearing, and it was only when I went to Australia with my partner and some friends that I jumped off a boat and swam a mile to a reef and back."*

Even so what he had done did not really hit Stephen until several weeks later, when he was watching a television programme on phobias. "And I thought, oh God! It was such an effective clearing that I couldn't even remember I had a phobia in the first place, so it didn't even enter my head. In fact I remember on the boat the divemaster said, 'Do you want any buoyancy aids' and things – everybody else had them except me and all I could say was, 'No, but I do want to wear fins because if there's something at the bottom I want to get down to see it': I could get down to it easier. That's not something that comes from somebody who's got a phobia about deep water...y'know, I was actually trying to get *down* there!"

The experience, I said to Stephen, must have resonated for him on other levels. How did he now see himself as operating in a way that previously he might have considered as out of his depth?

Stephen: Well for instance, running a magical lodge, being a magus, being a SOL supervisor. I mean, I wouldn't have dreamt of doing that at all; I would have had all sorts of personal considerations like I'm not good enough and I certainly wouldn't know how to do that; I'm not the sort of person who takes on that sort of responsibility. I'm much more willing now to try things out without actually having been told how to do them.

SVN: It's like you're in really deep water now, with what you're doing

Stephen: And it feels comfortable. I've found a faith; there's a certain... like a bedrock of faith with me now; I know that I will be guided; I know I have the capabilities and wherewithal to do things, whereas before I might not have done it.

So struck was Stephen by how effective the emotional clearing had been for him that he wanted to be able to do it for other people. He saw how it could help them to advance on the spiritual path.

> *"I saw it like on the spine...y'know, where you've got the spiritual and the mental, the emotional and the physical; if there are any blockages on any one of those levels, say kind of behaviour or whatever, then it's not surprising people can't get up to the spiritual levels if they've got something major that's stopping the free flow of energy, whoever they are, no matter how highly they think they've evolved spiritually."*

Stephen subsequently went on to train as a Master NLP Practitioner and hypnotherapist and now works with members of his lodge and private clients to clear any emotional blocks they may have. He uses a mixture of personal development and magical techniques in his work.

> *"Before I meet them, I always meet their higher self, so I have a meditation in the morning because I know that the higher aspect of whoever my client's going to be, will know exactly what that person needs. I might write down physically what I'm going to do with the person, think, that's going to be the*

best thing for them, but very often I'm moved to do something completely different."

There are many significators in Stephen's chart – three planets in earthy Taurus, maternal Cancer on the Midheaven, the rising Moon, an angular Neptune that opposes his Mercury and Venus in Taurus, and rules his Mars South Node in Pisces – that describe a compassionate, sensitive, nurturing and caring energy that well equips him to help his fellow human beings to break through the barriers that impede spiritual progress, and thus achieve their highest potential.

Inner balance and harmony

But what of Monica? How had she fared on the chosen road? How had her life changed, in both the magical and mundane sense? With Jupiter toing and froing over her natal Mercury it's hardly surprising that Monica experienced the aftermath of her First Degree initiation as a time of expansion, of opportunities to do other things. Her lodge put on their first really big workshop and at work there were openings for advancement. It was 'a very hectic time' but the inner balance and harmony that the First Degree initiate is expected to develop helped Monica to cope. "I think that does come in more strongly...I mean, y'know, bills still have to get paid, you still have to drive to work and all that kind of stuff, but there's just a calmer acceptance and harmony within."

Monica went on:-

> *"I think one of the other realisations that the First Degree at least provides to me and maybe to some others is this isn't the first time; we're taught that it takes three lives to make an initiate, so obviously we've been here before and past life recall has come in more strongly – I remember bits and pieces of past lives, I do; now whether they're my past lives?...y'know, I can be a sceptic and say maybe not, maybe I'm just tapping into some subconscious forces out there, but I do have a feeling that there is a continuity of spirit, of life; so time is an illusion, in many ways, and things happen in their own time; there is enough time to get everything done and I'm not going to just panic about being three minutes late for work; maybe I needed to be three minutes late for work for something else to happen. So that inner balance and inner harmony is tied up with the physical world, but on another level it's kind of separate from it. But the physical world can do all that hurrying and scurrying and running around crazy and it's like but for everything there is a*

> *plan – I* believe *there is a plan, and I believe there's enough time to get that plan accomplished and there are forces and forms who are helping move things in the right places and ways to get that accomplished, and I'm gonna go with that flow whenever I have the chance to do that."*

Anyone with Saturn strong in their chart, or Capricorn, the sign that it rules, is acutely aware of time; of the passage of time; of the finiteness of time; of the pressure to get things done before time runs out. Saturn of course is Lord of Time and of Fate; the Roman name for the planet is Cronus, from the Greek *chronos* which means 'time'. And in Monica's chart, as we have seen, Capricorn is the sign on the Ascendant, with Saturn in a prominent position making a number of key contacts to other planets.

When I asked Monica to look back on her First Degree initiation she said something that I think many of you reading this book will be able to relate to, as you perhaps contemplate taking such a step yourselves:-

> *"…even though…there was still that trepidation that maybe I really wasn't ready, I think it was probably the right time …I remember talking to Dolores …and Dolores saying, you're acting just like a horse before a big jump, you're just shying at the jump – just leap across, it's OK. And that leap, I think is what a First Degree initiation is – it's that leap across the unknown."*

Spiritual role

As Dolores said in her introduction the First Degree initiation changes you physically, mentally, emotionally and spiritually. It prepares you for your particular spiritual role; very often this involves putting gifts you may have and skills you've acquired in the mundane world in the service of a higher cause; taking them up a level, in other words.

As a child Monica had enjoyed colouring, drawing, painting and making things: she has three planets in artistic Cancer, ruled by the Moon; as well as an emphasis on creative Leo, ruled by the Sun. The Sun closely conjoins Uranus in the sixth house of work and service; Uranus rules the North Node in Aquarius in the first house; and the Moon falls in Sagittarius in the 11th house. Uranus, Aquarius and the 11th house are all to do with groups, so a very strong astrological message is being stated here: that the higher purpose of this incarnation is for Monica to serve the group in some way. "I do agree with that," said Monica, "and I do feel that part of my spiritual journey is to be a supporting member of the group and whatever that group wants me to do is what I'm going to do for them, so for my lodge I do arts and crafts and sewing and stuff like that; for SOL I'm a supervisor and help out with workshops."

Monica's contribution is an essential ingredient of the workshops she attends: her costumes, head-dresses and props are made with a love, care and attention to detail that enhances the experience for every participant. Truly she serves and supports the group.

'To thine own self be true'[10]

So what advice can I give you, who may be taking your first steps on the path? Or perhaps considering venturing further along it? I began this chapter with one old saying, 'know thyself', and now I shall end it with another: to thine own self be true.

It will take courage, a strong will and an open heart. Courage to meet and pass tests of character, integrity and intent to serve; a strong will to press on, when alone and disillusioned; and an open heart, to give and receive the power of love.

Do you still wish to continue? Then read on.

THE SECOND DEGREE

The Candidates

By Stephanie

Paul, Master of Patterns

> *"For me the Second Degree is a no-turning-back point. For me it was all or nothing at that point."*

We met Paul briefly in the last chapter as the organiser of a workshop that Stephen had attended. At the time Paul was a First Degree initiate of some three-and-a-half years' standing and only two months away from being initiated into the Second Degree. This took place at a workshop of Arthurian ritual of such intensity and power that it left Paul 'shaken up, turned inside out and put back together again in a new and wonderful way'.

How did Paul get to this point in his life? What equipped him to advance to the Second Degree? What were the early influences that helped to shape his destiny? For some clues to the answers, let us turn to his natal chart (*fig 8*).

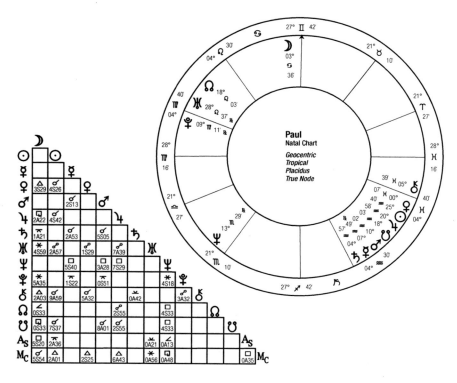

Fig 8

Paul has a very striking chart, on several counts. He has no less than five planets in Aquarius, including Mercury, which rules his chart; as well as the South Node of the Moon. Interestingly all these planets are in the house traditionally associated with his opposite sign, Leo – the solar fifth house of creativity and self-expression. So a major theme of Paul's life is his role as an individual vis-à-vis the group: the North Node in Leo, together with Uranus which rules all his planets in Aquarius indicate that in this life Paul is to lead, whereas in a previous life or lives he has probably shared decision-making and responsibility with his peers or brothers. I felt very strongly when I studied Paul's chart that in another incarnation he had been a member of a spiritual brotherhood of some kind. On another occasion, when I did a personal reading for him, I had a mental picture of him 'stepping out of line'. This of course can be taken in more than one way: to step out of the line is to put yourself forward, to draw attention to yourself; to step out of line is also not to conform, a key characteristic of independent-minded Aquarius.

Left to such a conglomeration of planets in Aquarius, Paul might well have pursued knowledge ruthlessly for its own sake, but the Moon in its own sign of Cancer, dominating the chart from the tenth house, tells a different story, describing a man to whom family life is important. Paul is married, with two young children.

Venus, similarly well-placed in sister Water sign, Pisces rules the ninth house, suggesting a religious inheritance from the female side of the family. Paul describes his mother's family as 'good C of E[11] people', particularly his grandmother who insisted he went to Sunday school when he was a child.

Both Venus and the Moon form a triangle in the water signs with Neptune in Scorpio, a key planet in Paul's chart because it's also at right angles to the Moon's Nodes, as well as all his planets in Aquarius. Neptune, as we have seen, rules other dimensions and other worlds and one of the keywords most often associated with it is 'mystery'. In Paul's chart Neptune rules the sixth house of work and the seventh of relationships; as well as Venus, which in turn rules part of the eighth house of the occult as well as the ninth. It is but a short leap from 'mystery' to 'Mysteries' as in Western Mysteries which, as we shall see later on in this chapter, Paul realised his life was 'irrevocably tied to' after he had been initiated into the Second Degree.

There is just one more feature of Paul's chart I want to draw attention to at this stage and that is a pattern of energy formed by his planets in early Aquarius at 150 degree angle to his Moon in Cancer or Pluto in Virgo, with the former planet sextile the other. This is known as a *yod*, with the planets at the apex of the configuration – Mercury, Mars and Saturn – known as the finger of fate or finger of God. Because of the strain of the angle, the individual in whose chart this configuration appears is under pressure to act; the area of the chart to which the 'finger' – or in Paul's case more like a bunched fist, with so many planets involved – is pointing, will be the arena in which his destiny is played out. In Paul's chart it is the 11th house of the group, with the sign of Leo on the cusp in which both his North Node and Uranus fall. In setting up his own magical school – a long-held ambition of Paul's – he will realise a destiny he may have incarnated to fulfil.

So how and when did this destiny begin to unfold?

It was Stuart Wilde, author of *The Taos Quintet* and other books on self-empowerment who, Paul says, 'really put me on to the whole magical thing.' This was back in 1990 and led Paul to Neuro-Linguistic Programming (NLP) and master trainer Tad James. Then in early 1991 Paul started reading Dion Fortune[12], specifically *The Training and Work of an Initiate* and *Esoteric Orders and their Work*. Saturn had arrived in Aquarius and Paul was experiencing his first Saturn return. During the course of its three-year stay in this sign, of which it is the ancient ruler, Saturn would transit all of Paul's planets in Aquarius one by one. When it got up to the degree of his Sun, in December 1993, he went to one of Dolores's workshops and 'really connected with her'. Paul had met his teacher.

In 1994 Paul, by now a certified NLP Practitioner, left the SOL course to study Huna, the ancient Hawaiian system of magic and healing. A few years later he returned to the SOL course and was initiated into the First Degree in September 1999. A reminder here that in April 1995 Uranus entered Aquarius, not to leave until December 2003; to be followed in January 1998 by Neptune, which is not due to leave Aquarius until February 2012. These are massive transits for Paul, with the former planet ruling half his chart and the latter squaring it. Together they would rock the very foundation on which his sense of self was built and realign it on the most subtle of levels.

Initiation on the astral

> *"Anubis appeared through the Western Gate and walked round the edge of the temple, and then during the meditation he walked up to me – and I distinctly remember it – he placed his hands on my head and there was this huge kind of flash of white light. It was a huge influx of energy because I really felt it and I really felt it shifted me somehow consciously."*

That's as much as Paul remembers of what Dolores later confirmed had been an initiation into the Second Degree on the astral. It took place on the occasion of the consecration of Paul's temple on 24 June 2002 and coincided almost exactly to the minute with that night's Full Moon, all the more powerful for occurring only three days after the Sun's entry into Cancer, which marks the summer solstice in the northern hemisphere. With the Full Moon falling directly opposite Paul's natal Moon in Cancer, small wonder that he experienced its energy so directly and felt that it had changed him.

Paul thought that he would be initiated into the Second Degree at a workshop on the Black and White Isis, held the following November. But much to his disappointment, he wasn't; instead he found himself officiating at someone else's Second Degree initiation. Dolores told him that it was not the right time for him and added, mysteriously, that he had more work to do before he received the Second Degree. Just before we leave the Temple of the Black and White Isis, I want to mention another ritual that was enacted that weekend, in which Paul played the part of Master of Patterns, a role that required him to weave a pattern of joy and laughter, health and contentment that would bind together all those present. It is this name that I have chosen to call him, because with all his planets in Aquarius, opposite his North Node and squared by Neptune – the central configuration of his chart – Paul has a unique ability to compartmentalise and systematise information, and thus to maintain and sustain many different kinds of relationships at many different levels simultaneously.

But what of this work that Paul had still to do before he was initiated into the Second Degree? That Christmas of 2002, some 'serious personal stuff' came up for him.

> *"There was a whole pile of stuff around whether the relationship with my other half was what I wanted, because it was clear to me at that point she wasn't my magical partner. So that was a problem for me, because I wanted to be in a relationship with someone who was both my life partner and my magical partner. And I had to go through a whole process of accepting that that wasn't going to be the case."*

In coming to terms with this realisation, Paul spent a lot of time 'clearing his emotional stuff' with his NLP training partner. It all came to a head towards the end of January 2003, when transiting Mercury stationed, or came to a standstill in Capricorn, the sign opposite his Moon. An internal process that had begun with Mercury's entry into this sign – intercepted in Paul's chart and therefore not easily accessible by him – in early December 2002, was now complete and he was ready to go forward. In less than six weeks' time Paul would be initiated into the Second Degree.

The events that took place in the second half of 2002 and early 2003 – the consecration of Paul's temple, the workshop on the Black and White Isis, the clearing of negative emotions – in effect the build-up to Paul's Second Degree, have to be viewed against the backdrop of the slow-moving Uranus and Neptune transits. Throughout 2002 Uranus was passing backwards and forwards over his Sun, while Neptune was doing likewise over his Mars. Between them these two planets were redefining Paul's sense of identity and his purpose for being here.

"It was during that period that I finally began to realise that in keeping my own company going, it was almost like flogging a dead horse. I think it was towards that time I finally got the message that this is not your path: your path is to do the spiritual stuff."

Transiting Jupiter had also moved into Paul's opposite sign, Leo on 1 August, soon to be within orb of his North Node, revealing the direction his life was to take. On 4 December the planet of growth and opportunity stationed retrograde in the same degree and almost the same minute, a powerful nudge that Paul had to look within before he could proceed further on his path. "I'm absolutely convinced that had I not dealt with all of those things then, the initiation would not have taken, because there would have been too many blocks emotionally to allow that energy to go through."

Emotional clearing is something we touched on with Stephen in the previous chapter. I asked Paul what was so important about it, particularly for people on the magical path.

"The negative emotions, in my understanding and experience, block energy flow through the body. If we are wanting to raise our level of vibration, which is essentially what initiation does – at least on one level that's what it does – then we need to take out of our nervous system anything that's going to stop that vibration from being raised. Negative emotions specifically, and limiting beliefs, block the flow of energy because they limit the level of vibration. They're like clogging up the system. If you think of it in terms of an Eastern model, of energy rising up the spine, then when the energy of initiation rises, it will hit any blocks in the nervous system that are there and those blocks are negative emotions – anger, fear, sadness, hurt, guilt – that stuff. So that's why when people go through initiatory experiences, their stuff comes up, quite literally."

In her introduction Dolores said that the Lords of Light 'will move you around quite ruthlessly to achieve their aims'. I would add, from a psychological point of view, that they will tap into your personal 'stuff' or complexes time and again in order to help you to evolve into a higher being. The more self-aware you are, the more complete you are with your early life experiences in particular, the less traumatic this process will be and the quicker you will advance along the path.

Within the Castle of the Grail

"I thought Galahad was a bit of a nancy boy, really."

"Lancelot, I thought, he's the knight who had the affair with Guinevere."

It was the week before *Within the Castle of the Grail*, a workshop that took place in Wales from Friday, 28 February to Sunday, 2 March 2003 and Paul and another man, Gavin had just been informed by Dolores that they would be playing the parts of Lancelot and Galahad, Knights of King Arthur's Round Table respectively. It was in these roles that the two men would be initiated into the Second Degree on Sunday morning. And so, with little idea of what to expect, Gavin and Paul made their separate ways to the workshop. At this point Paul was unaware that as Lancelot, he would be playing father to Gavin's Galahad, his son.

Friday night

When Gavin and Paul arrived at the workshop late on Friday, they found that they had been allocated a room together and within the space of a few hours started developing a 'tremendous bond', even although they didn't know each other very well. They went round together, jokingly referring to each other as 'Dad' and 'Son' and helping each other to learn their lines. It soon became clear to both of them that the focus of the whole weekend was on them and their relationship, both actual and mythological.

"I remember even sitting down with Gavin and saying, 'I feel kind of bad because I'm not doing what I'm supposed to be doing, and that's paying attention to Guinevere'. In the same way I didn't connect with Arthur either, although Lancelot is supposed to be Arthur's best friend – I mean, I just simply really wasn't in that space."

In addition, on a different level Paul started to identify the relationship between Gavin and himself with that between his own son and himself, so successfully that when a Mass of the Grail was enacted on Sunday and Galahad had to die in order to withdraw with the Grail to the higher realms, he could not hold back the tears: he had lost the son he had only just found and with him, the chance to see the glory of the Grail unveiled.

Saturday afternoon

The Grail Mass was the culmination of Gavin and Paul's Second Degree initiation, which really began on Saturday afternoon, when Galahad was presented to King Arthur's court by his mother, Elaine, the Maid of Astolat. This is the first Lancelot learns that he has a son. In her evocative retelling of the Arthurian myth, *The Legends of King Arthur*, Rosemary Sutcliff describes how Elaine, for love of Lancelot and with the help of her old nurse, who knew how to spice a man's wine so that he thought he saw what he did not, seduced Lancelot. Enchanted as he was, Lancelot believed he was lying with his love, Queen Guinevere. In the cold clear light of morning he realises his mistake and flees. But the spell had done its work and Elaine was to bear him a son, Galahad, the Grail Prince.

Later that day there came the accusation of Mordred – King Arthur's son by his half-sister, Morgause (conceived in another act of deception that was to prove the undoing of both Arthur and his kingdom) – against Guinevere and Lancelot, when he makes public their affair.

What was the reaction of Lancelot/Paul as he watched the shadow fall over Arthur's shining court?

> *"I saw the complete mess that Lancelot had created, quite unwittingly, really, of the relationship between him and Guinevere and Arthur, and the repercussions it had for the kingdom that he clearly hadn't realised or thought about at the time."*

Whether Lancelot acted out of complete ignorance, or lust, or jealousy, we shall never know. In Sutcliff's rendering of the myth, Lancelot was fostered as a child by Nimuë, Lady of the Lake. Although afterwards he could remember nothing of that time passed within the Hollow Hills, he was forever marked by it. And the values of Faery[13] are not those of mortals and those who find their way to its enchanted realm cannot be held to account in the same way.

Saturday evening

In preparation for his knighting on Saturday evening Galahad/Gavin had to undertake a four-hour fast and vigil in the temple, during which the knights standing guard over him would be changed every 15 minutes. But Paul, by now well and truly in the grip of his character's archetype, insisted on being present the whole time. Galahad/Gavin knelt before the altar and Lancelot/Paul stood immediately behind him, sword in hand, with a supporter either side.

"That was the point at which I really felt we started to make a much stronger connection, me and Gavin – not physically, but if I can use the word, energetically... I was conscious, as I stood behind him, visualising energy flowing through me and into him, as a way of supporting him in what he was doing, of looking round and seeing a row of knights down either side of the temple. And they were really, really vivid: all in chain mail with white tabards with red crosses on them. It wasn't just me who saw them and I'm absolutely convinced that they were there."

The vigil was an initiation both for Gavin in the role of Galahad, who was knighted immediately afterwards and for Paul in the role of Lancelot. The following morning the two men would be initiated together into the Second Degree. As they prepared to go to bed that night, Gavin said to Paul, "You realise this is going to be a really emotional experience for both of us, don't you?"

Sunday morning

By the time they rose the following morning, the Moon had moved into Pisces; the next day, Monday 3 March there was a New Moon in this most sensitive and emotional sign of the zodiac. So the whole weekend was held in the last days of the waning Moon, the darkest and most magical time of its cycle. On Friday when Gavin and Paul had met in the fellowship of the Round Table, the Moon had been in Aquarius, the sign of brotherhood. That day and the next, they had learnt their lines; now they had to play them for real.

Half an hour after the ritual for initiation into the Second Degree began, Dolores tied the silver cord round Gavin and Paul's waists. As the biwheel chart with Paul's planets on the inside and those for the tying of the cord shows, it was a serene moment for him: the Moon was in harmonious relationship to his Moon in Cancer, in the same degree and almost the same minute (*fig 9*).

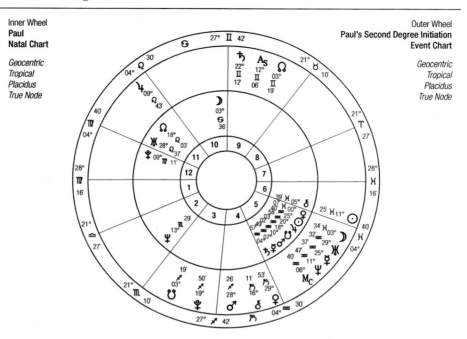

Fig 9

The Initiation Jupiter, retrograde in Leo was also opposite his planets in early Aquarius; shortly it would go direct and pass over his North Node for the second time. The first time it had gone over, in December 2002 Paul had realised that his path lay in a spiritual direction. 'I suspected that before,' he said, 'but I didn't really know it.' For Paul the Second Degree initiation was a 'no-turning-back point':

> *"Up until that point you could have said no, I've had enough now, I've done my bit, I've learnt interesting things, but that's as far as I go. I think, once you take the Second Degree, it is definitely a no-going-back. I know that people say that of the Third Degree, but I think that process starts in the Second. For me, it was all or nothing at that point."*

It was an important moment in the magical destinies of both men, from which they would not look back.

The Grail Mass

The Grail Mass followed immediately on Gavin and Paul's Second Degree initiation and to have some appreciation of its emotional impact on the two men, we must bear in mind that the Second Degree entails a subtle tuning of the vibration to a higher level: what Dolores calls in the next section, *The Silver Cord*, 'turning up the volume'. This tweak of the controls, if you like, may be so imperceptible as to escape notice, but it is no less powerful for that. In this highly sensitised state then, the two men went into the Grail Mass where, as Galahad and Lancelot, they must take leave of each other forever.

The Grail Mass was a culmination not only of the initiation that had just taken place, it was also, on a personal level, a deeply painful culmination for Lancelot/Paul: having only just been reunited with the son he never knew he had, he must now relinquish Galahad/Gavin to a higher cause and a higher realm. As the Grail Prince, it falls to Galahad to withdraw the Grail, until such time as humanity is ready to receive the priceless gift of 1,000 years of peace and harmony.

> *"As I stepped up to Galahad to say my goodbyes, my entire being was screaming, 'No! This cannot be!' I was amazed at the depth of my emotions. It was as if my own, real son was dying and I was saying goodbye to him. First my voice broke and then the tears came. I understood at every level of my being what Lancelot had gone through. I was Lancelot and here was his son."*

Galahad was dead, Camelot had fallen, the Grail was veiled from mortal view and with it, the bright promise of a new and happier age.

Erica, Keeper of the Sacred Flame

> *"The most intense feeling…was as though a dam had broken in my mind. There was a constant flow of thought and inspiration and I felt that anything was possible."*

'Much that was very special has happened to me since my Second Degree and begun to happen before that,' Erica emailed me in response to the invitation to be interviewed for this book. When I turned up at her house there was another woman there, Yolande, a friend of Erica's from the SOL lodge to which they both belong. I smiled to myself, knowing that Erica has the Moon in Gemini which is of course a dual sign. Yolande was present throughout the interview and would occasionally interject, to help Erica out or to clarify a point. Yolande is from Jamaica, where they have a saying, 'Out of many one people' and is of mixed African, Irish, Scottish and Asian descent.

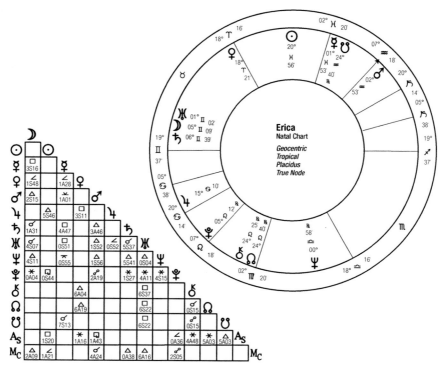

Fig 10

I mention this because it's central to an understanding of Erica's natal chart (*fig 10*), which is where we begin this study of a female candidate for the Second Degree. Erica has not only the Moon, but also Saturn and Uranus in Gemini in the 12th house, an area of the chart associated mundanely with ancestry and institutions, but magically with the astral, the spiritual and all that which is invisible or intangible. Erica also has Gemini rising, which makes Mercury, the planet of the mind and communication, the ruler of her chart. Mercury is in Pisces and sits with the South Node in Aquarius in the 10th house.

Just from this we can straightaway tell that communication is a dominant theme of Erica's life. In emotional Pisces however, Mercury is not at its most rational or communicative, at least not in the ordinary sense. I have noticed with people who have Mercury in Pisces, that they have an uncanny ability to read other people's minds; that they 'have an ear', which makes them sensitive to sound(s) that other people do not hear or are not influenced by to the same extent. It doesn't take much to see how Mercury in Pisces has come to be associated with telepathic communication, or communication with Spirit, that is, with beings in other dimensions, dimensions other than the physical.

In the same email Erica had warned me that she had 'a terrible fault of becoming tongue-tied when put on the spot': her Mercury is square, or at right angles, to that Moon Saturn Uranus in Gemini, indicating that she experiences an internal struggle to express her feelings. At one point in the interview she said, 'I can write them, but I can't speak them'. In one of a series of booklets she has written (of which more later) she says:

> *"I love the concept of telepathic communication, without the spoken word. Telepathy is of course how Spirit will normally speak to one. Sometimes it is so subtle, like a thought woven into your own and you can hardly tell the difference, but at other times you hear the words as it were. I feel that telepathy is the true language. We have to learn to use the spoken word here and that has often tied me up in knots, because it is difficult for me to speak all that I know."*

Especially as Erica's Mercury is conjunct the South Node, an indication that she has incarnated with knowledge to share from a past life or lives; and that in this life she is challenged to express, with her Moon (Saturn) Uranus square her North Node in Leo.

Remembering and re-membering

It was in June 2002 that Erica learned she was to be initiated into the Second Degree in November of that year. The same month she began a dialogue in writing with someone she'd just met that she felt paved the way for what was to come. It opened her up, not so much to new ideas, but to 'things I already knew', in what she called a process of remembering: 'in both senses of the word, of remembering something you've actually forgotten, and of re-membering, the coming together with other parts of yourself'. It was a process that Erica found very exciting, a word that resonated with me as it usually means that transiting Uranus is active in the chart.

Sure enough, at the beginning of June Uranus, the planet that rules not only Erica's South Node in Aquarius, but also her Midheaven and Mars (in an area of the chart associated with knowledge of higher things), had stationed, prior to going into reverse for the next five months. A process was under way, one that would take Erica all the way up to her Second Degree initiation. The action of Uranus is to awaken; in Erica's case, to a knowledge of what she called her true self. Could she give me an idea of this true self? I asked.

Silence

Yolande: Can I say something?

Erica: You say something. We've shared a tremendous amount, Yolande and I.

Yolande: You're talking about your cosmic roots, aren't you?

Erica: Yes that's right. I'd forgotten the cosmic me I suppose.

SVN: The cosmic me? Now you'll have to explain that...

Erica: Oh dear. Oh dear. How would I explain that?

Yolande: You can.

Erica: Well it's the godself; the self that's capable of anything, the self that knows everything...

SVN: Is it also the self that feels connected to the Universe, everybody else...

Erica: Yes, very much so, yeah...exactly...

How had Erica come to 'forget' this self? To forget, as she put it, that 'one doesn't have a right to be what one truly is'? At this point on the tape she referred to certain 'experiences in the world' and said, 'You can get very much put down...not given certain opportunities for things...'. Erica is in her 60s, divorced, with a grown-up daughter and two grand-children. In an email she wrote to me later she described emerging from a couple of relationships as 'pretty fragmented'. Hence the need for re(-)membrance, in both a mundane and a spiritual sense. " The accent for me is on the spiritual, however this is impossible without first re-membering the mundane self – to a certain degree at least. One works at this through the SOL course anyway and it all begins to come together."

The most interesting thing about this process, from an astrological point of view, is that at around the same time as transiting Uranus was awakening Erica to a knowledge of her true self, her Moon progressed into Leo. Leo is ruled by the Sun and its sense of self is therefore perhaps stronger and more whole than that of any other sign.

On 4 November 2002, 12 days before Erica was due to be initiated into the Second Degree, Uranus stationed again, this time to go forwards, in the same degree as Erica's South Node, which is of course conjunct her Mercury. Erica was on the brink of a breakthrough.

The breaking of the dam

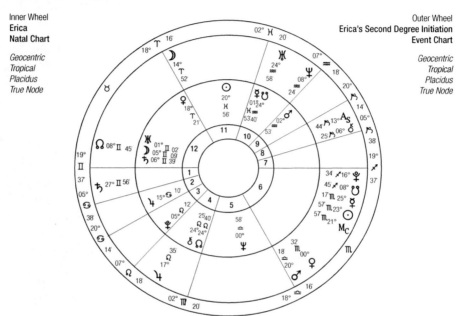

Fig 11

In the event it occurred not at the ritual itself, but shortly afterwards. That Erica was due for something of this kind is evident from a look at the biwheel chart with her natal planets on the inside and those for her Second Degree initiation on the outside (*fig 11*). The Initiation Sun and Mercury in Scorpio, a sign that is intercepted in Erica's chart, squares her nodal axis and Mercury and opposes her (Moon Saturn) Uranus, forming a Grand Cross, a configuration of pressure and power, from the sixth house of work and service. In fact no less than five of the initiation planets fall in Erica's natal sixth and her nodes are heavily aspected, by almost all the initiation planets.

One of these, Jupiter stationed a few degrees off her North Node at the beginning of December; at around the same time Mars entered Scorpio. Together they triggered what Erica described as 'a new surge of inner activity'. Certainly at the end of December she embarked on a series of communications with an entity she refers to simply as 'my Spirit Friend'. Although not prepared to go into detail, Erica described him as 'kind, humorous, patient with my endless questions, inspiring and very encouraging'. In all Erica had 16 sessions with this Spirit, conducted 'through the vehicle of a gifted friend'. During the 1980s she had spent many years involved with psychics and mediums and had always wished for communication of this quality.

The Spirit also offered to give Erica a healing for ME, an illness she had struggled with for several years. She felt the effects immediately. 'The most intense feeling in this respect,' she wrote, 'was as though a dam had broken in my mind. There was a constant flow of thought and inspiration and I felt that anything was possible.'

It was a very special time for Erica, marked by many 'strange experiences' the most significant of which I quote from below.

> *"I lie in my bed on New Year's morning 2004. I am wide awake. I am not meditating nor thinking of related matters and neither do I have a hangover after the night before's celebrations. Suddenly I am aware of a shift of consciousness, like the breaking through into another dimension of being. I am watching a scene in front of me as well as being within the scene myself. Visually the picture lacks clarity and I do not hear words, both of which are my usual means of Spirit communication. What is particularly strong however, is the intensity of feeling generated by this experience.*

> *"I am watching a Great Being of Light, of an appropriate likeness for me, holding in its arms and close to its heart, a tiny Being of Light. But as I watch this I feel intensely from the perspective of that tiny Being, which is part of the greater self that is I. I cannot get enough, so to speak and all I wish to do is to bury myself deeper and deeper within this Great Being. I am aware that nothing else matters, for in truth there is nothing else for me. All my usual fears of losing my independence and freedom have vanished, because these are of no importance here. I am finally home and at peace, after a very long and tiring journey. This is where I want to be, forever a part of this Great Being of Light, safe, warm and loved."*

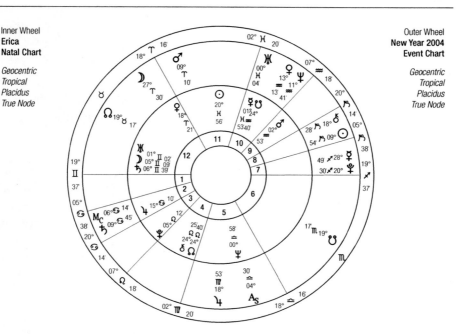

Fig 12

I would expect some pretty powerful astrology to be around for an experience such as this to occur and when I checked the ephemeris I was not disappointed. By January 2004 Uranus had reentered Pisces and as the biwheel chart with Erica's planets on the inside and those for New Year's Day 2004 on the outside shows, was less than two degrees off her Mercury: the very words she uses, 'the sudden shift of consciousness, like the breaking through into another dimension' exactly describe the action of The Awakener (Uranus) on the planet of the mind (Mercury).

At the same time Jupiter, the planet that rules Sagittarius, the sign on the Descendant in Erica's chart, stationed two days later opposite her Sun, square to her Ascendant; while transiting Mercury and Pluto were to be found in her seventh house. The way had been opened for Erica to have a direct experience of a great and powerful Being which she was later to describe as 'union with the Divine'. Her Spirit Friend told her afterwards that this was an encounter with her 'Father'; with her Sun in Pisces aspected by Jupiter, Neptune and Pluto, Erica is particularly disposed to an encounter with a being of this kind.

The intensity of feeling accompanying this experience suggests that it was deeply cathartic for Erica, as indeed it was: a few nights before she had gone through a crisis 'of just not being able to reach that which I desperately wanted to reach. I was in tears and was genuinely prepared to offer everything I had if that was what "they" wanted of me. I even said that "they" could take my life if "they" wanted.'

The whole experience felt to Erica like 'coming home' and interestingly was preceded by a move in which she did literally come home, to the place where she was born.

Encouraging people to explore

If we are to take Uranus transiting over Erica's South Node and Mercury as the main astrological significator of 'the dam breaking in her mind', facilitating the process of remembrance or the flow of ideas and thoughts from the past, it's hardly surprising that she should start writing – something, she said, she would not have dared to do before – about her experiences. She has produced what she calls an exploratory series of booklets and explains the thinking behind them:-

> *"There's a lot of things you can't teach, because people have to learn from their own experience. You can encourage people towards having these experiences; you can describe your own experiences; you can encourage people by saying, 'Look, it can happen to you – you don't just have to read about it in books, this can happen.' That's what I'm doing this writing for – I call it encouraging people to explore."*

Yolande: I don't want to speak, but –

(*Yolande was born the day after a Full Moon, so the impetuousness of her Sun and Mercury in Aries is balanced by the tact and sensitivity of her Moon and Neptune in Libra.*)

Erica: Yolande knows me well and can sometimes express things better in words than I can.

Yolande: It's nice to be humble but sometimes we have to speak out... The other thing you do that I've observed is it's almost as if you want to do it for yourself, but you're more inclined to encourage others to go and get what you need –

Erica: It's easier to encourage others rather than trying to go and get something for yourself – I mean it doesn't seem quite so selfish...

Yolande: There are things I do and I know I can do them, but I keep them very quiet, but then sometimes they have to come out and you've encouraged me in that…it's facilitating –

SVN: How has Erica facilitated you, Yolande? What is it that she's helped you to bring out?

Yolande: Well I think within the group – I'm a new member of Lodge, very new member – but because we've been corresponding and stuff, Erica knows my intuitive abilities… This is what Spirit wanted ultimately, for me to be in the position of Seer, and I would never – I mean, you don't, do you; you get placed where you need to be and that's where you are, but I think she insisted, for some reason and that's what I mean about fighting for others – not fighting, but you know, coming forward and insisting and then it happened –

Erica: Yeah, you drew that lot for Seer –

Yolande: I know that, but I would never have said to anyone in the group that I had this ability…

Erica: I like to see people being able to use their abilities to the full – share them to the benefit of other people.

Erica has Mars, the Midheaven and the South Node all in altruistic Aquarius; as we have seen she has a gift for mediumship, but she has another perhaps even more rare and special gift, and that is the gift of facilitating the gifts of others.

I've quoted from this part of the interview in full because it illustrates so well how the nodal dynamic works in Erica's chart. Her Mercury conjunct the South Node gives her a kind of bird's-eye view of the group and what it needs from each of its members in order to function as a whole. However her North Node is in self-expressive, dramatic Leo, which requires her to perform a special and important role in the group.

In the SOL lodge of which she is a founding member Erica has two roles, the first as an upholder of power, which she defined as:-

> *"An upholder of power has to be strong in themselves; I think they have to have quite a wide understanding of what's going on, the energies; they don't have to stick out or be noisy – in fact it suits me, because I'm quite often quiet… It's very much a behind-the-scenes sort of thing, and people don't notice what*

you're doing or how you are."

But Erica's central role in Lodge is as Keeper of the Sacred Flame. If you look at her chart you'll see that her North Node in Leo is closely conjunct Chiron. Leo is of course a Fire sign and the glyph for Chiron looks like the letter 'k' over a circle – the symbolism perfectly describes her role.

Chiron

In Greek mythology Chiron was the Wounded Healer, half-man, half-centaur, who could not heal the accidental wound inflicted upon him by Hercules, but who adopted the role of tutor and mentor to many of its most famous heroes, among them Asclepius, Achilles and Jason. The 'k' stands for the Greek word *kheir* meaning 'hand': it is with the hand that we turn a key in a lock and open a door; as symbolised by Chiron to a new awareness, born of an acknowledgment and acceptance of the psychic wounds we bear as an inevitable consequence of being mortal; and thus to wholeness, as symbolised by the circle in the glyph.

Both Erica's Second Degree initiation and the New Year's Day vision were marked astrologically by stations of Jupiter: in the case of the former, a few degrees off her Chiron North Node in Leo; in the case of the latter opposite her Sun in Pisces. The Divine Father had shown himself in order to salve the wounds inflicted by his earthly counterparts, thus releasing Erica to teach her own unique brand of wisdom.

The Sacred Flame

> *"For me the sacred flame is a flame that doesn't flicker. A steady flame. It can be made to flicker, but only through will. It musn't flicker without it being your will. The flame is in the centre – the centre of the group, the centre of each one of us."*

The sacred flame is a subject that Erica's Spirit Friend told her to investigate. The result was a fifth booklet in her exploratory series called *Journey through the Sacred Flame*. It's longer than the others, running to 70 pages and was inspired by the magnificent images of spiral galaxies photographed by the Hubble telescope. In her introduction Erica says, 'I realised that I could not limit myself to the choice of a single flame of a single colour, for in truth flames are of all colours... To call a flame red, blue or yellow would be to limit it and a flame is unlimited and unlimiting.' The booklet consists of a series of pathworkings, or guided journeys using visualisation, through flames of different colours. In a postscript Erica describes the journey through the sacred flame as 'a journey of life, a journey of love and a journey of light': 'towards the true wisdom of illumination, without which we would never find our way home from the darkness and confusion of the labyrinth.'

A few days before Erica was given the role of Keeper of the Sacred Flame her Spirit Friend told her to learn the secrets of the sacred flame. This was in January 2004 when her progressed Moon was applying to her North Node and Chiron in Leo. In first learning and then teaching the secrets of the sacred flame, Erica could truly be said to be well on the way home herself.

The Silver Cord

By Dolores

Is the source of power different for the Second Degree?

The source of power is always the same, but in an adept it can be tuned to a higher vibration when needed. There is a certain level of awareness where the adept becomes a tool that the Lords of Light can use as a focal point, lifting or lowering the power as it may be needed. This occurs usually only when a person is dedicated to or bonded with a particular Master/school. Where the practitioner is working as a solo adept and therefore not committed to one Master, the internal power can be raised or lowered by the adept themselves. Again it depends on how much power is needed for a ritual or special working. However when one manipulates the power source for oneself, the tuning is not as fine or reliable as when done by a Master of Light.

So there are different levels of power available to an adept?

Yes, it is like a longbow. When not in use the bowstring is loosed otherwise it would lose its flexibility when needed. In the same way you never keep your power at full stretch all the time. To do so would exhaust you physically, mentally and spiritually. The method of raising or lowering is a personal thing and one learns it through trial and error...often painfully.

There is a natural level of power that flows through everyone, even those who are not part of the Mysteries, or even interested in them. It is that mysterious inner awareness that keeps us 'ticking over', like an engine idling. Disbelievers like to call it a sixth sense, women's intuition, a hunch or – the favourite word – coincidence. Nevertheless it exists and it can, with training, be brought to life and extended into a power that can be used in many ways, not all of them magically.

What exactly is a Second Degree initiation?

It is a natural progression that follows on from neophyte to First Degree and then to the Second. Not everyone is ready for it, or even wants it. Like the First, there is no set time; it is not a matter of saying, Oh, such and such a person has been with the school/order for so many years, let's give him or her a Second Degree. There is a feeling, an indefinable aura around those who are ready. It is sometimes difficult to pin down so one must be very careful; it is easy to make mistakes and that can mean difficulties for both the giver and the receiver. A Second Degree is also the time when the initiator (through the power and influence of the Master Contact of the school) must reach into the subtle levels of the person before them and turn up the volume, so to speak. The initiation itself increases the ability of the candidate to gradually receive contact with the Master at a higher level.

Boosting the seed to Second Degree

Essentially the seed a candidate is given in the First Degree holds the potential of all further degrees within itself. The Second and Third Degree initiations simply tune it to a finer vibration and upgrade its capacity to cope with a greater flow of power.

In the preceding chapter I told you that the seed once given can never be taken back; it will remain with the candidate until physical death when it joins with the returning spirit. At this point it continues to grow within the spiritual form in potential. When resting between lives the spirit reviews its past incarnation and with the help of guides and teachers decides what will be the best situation for its next life. The initiation seed plays an important part in this decision and its state of growth and its ongoing potential can influence the next life.

If that life is destined to include further work in the Mysteries the seed will be programmed to bring the person into situations where advancement will be possible. If a life of rest or of retribution has been decided on, it may lie dormant or feed strength and endurance into the spirit as needed.

Whatever is decided, that same seed will incarnate with the spirit into the new life. This is what is meant by 'once an initiate, always an initiate.' There are times when one meets a seemingly naïve person, maybe one who, though relatively uneducated, exhibits a wisdom and an understanding of the subtle life of the world around them. This may well be a life of rest after a past incarnation of strife and hardship. A life undertaken to refine the spirit or help a Master bring something of importance into the world.

What you see and feel is the brilliance of the seed shining through the physical shell and illuminating the space around itself.

Such a life may demand little of the seed or spirit, the person simply lives quietly, but nevertheless they are still an initiate and such a light cannot be completely hidden. Inevitably people will find their way to such a person to talk, to ask advice or simply to be within their auric shadow.

The enlargement of the initiate's auric field

Connected as it is to the etheric and to the physical energy pattern of the body, the aura is always affected by the act of initiation. Some people can achieve such an enlargement by drawing on an outside source of power, a relic, a sacred location, a jewel worn by someone of power, or more rarely, by the sheer force of the ego that desires such power. In the latter case the power does not last and inevitably fades after a while.

You can see this clearly in the swift rise and equally swift fall of some pop and film stars. The song or film that brings them instant fame increases the auric field for a time; if the adulation of the masses continues it may run for some time feeding off the hysteria going on around them. Then someone new comes along and the energy is withdrawn and everything falls down (a good description of the Struck Tower of the Tarot).

This is not to decry those singers, musicians and actors who deserve their fame by reason of genuine hard work in their chosen profession and who give such pleasure to those who watch and listen to them. Such people may well have chosen such a life for a purpose and may carry within them the all-important seed from a former life. Their lives may seem glamorous but are often filled with self-doubt and internal pain.

You will find people with extended auras in every walk of life, from those in high position, to those in the caring professions, academia, the arts and literature. If you can feel them before you see them, they have that extension. If they seem to surround you as you stand close to them, their aura is enclosing you. Ernest Butler[14] had an aura that could and did fill a hall or a church.

In these days few churchmen have a true vocation; the Church has become a profession rather than a calling, but there are still some genuine Christian priests who have this field of love. Moreover they exhibit that violet ray in their aura that enfolds all within its range.

Initiation begins the development of this extended aura and empowers it still further with each degree. Initiates often tell me they find people at work, at home and even strangers often start talking and opening up to them on things they have never shared with others. This is the power of the extended aura: it enfolds, supports, cleanses and calms troubled or needful souls. It is something every initiate should be prepared for and learn to cope with.

The Second Degree initiation

There is a tradition that the First Degree is offered, the Second may be asked for or you may be summoned to it. Let me clarify this. The First is offered because it is evident from the work, the behaviour and the dedication of the candidate that it is deserved and the student is at the right stage of development to cope with the responsibility it brings.

Sometimes, having taken the First and passed a fair time in further studies and the gaining of experience, a student will feel a sudden desire to go further. There may even be a sense of, 'I deserve this... Why can't I have it?'

All right – ask for it. Go to the head of your school or order and ask. You may be refused; you often are the first time because the teacher will want to test your resolve. If you go into a fit of sulks and resign, they were right to refuse you. If you accept that there is a reason for the refusal and wait, you will gain experience. Then perhaps in open Lodge you will be 'summoned' with due ceremony to attend the next meeting where your Second Degree will be given.

Sometimes you are summoned when you are totally unaware that you are being considered for it.

Seconds rarely carry the apprehension of the First and may often seem to be very low key, but the 'tuning' of the vibrations is very subtle here. It is what happens after the ceremony rather than the ceremony itself that causes the hiatus.

The ceremony often includes references to the establishing of the order or school and explanations may be given as to its origins and contacts. Officers may offer specific advice or demand certain actions of you. At your First you were asked for a coin: the obulos or fare for the ferryman at death; no initiate is ever refused passage across the divide between life and death; that coin is your key. You may have been asked for a drop of blood to put on your red cord. You will have received your magical ring, blessed and anointed, and your head and hands will have been oiled.

At the Second you may be crowned with light and cleansed with blessed water; you may receive a pair of slippers or sandals with which to walk between the worlds. Lastly you are given a silver cord to replace the red one and the medallion of the Second Degree is hung about your neck. Certain things differ from school to school, but some things run through all schools. The most important one is INTENT. Some schools have different coloured robes for the degrees; others simply use one colour but with different coloured cords.

The laying on of hands here is different in intent, for those hands have been primed beforehand by contact with the inner plane Master. The initiator's own seed will have been empowered and tuned and the vibrations from it will have been directed to the vagus nerve, where they rest. This is linked very powerfully to the heart in the physical, emotional and spiritual sense and when the hands are laid on you, those vibrations flow from the vagus down through the hands and into the candidate. At that moment the seed is retuned to its new level and vibrationary rate.

What does the ceremony mean?

It means the goal posts have been moved!! Things are not the same as they were. The red cord has gone and with it that responsibility for your own actions. From your First Degree initiation until now you have, or should have been taking full responsibility for what you have said, thought, done and caused to be. It is a source of pride to the wearer of a red cord that they have, since that time, accepted some of the pain of the Saviour of the Age, no matter how small. This arrangement has now ended.

With the acceptance of the silver cord you give the responsibility for your actions, words and deeds back to the Saviour of the Age!

What does this mean? It means that now you are fully aware of what responsibility means: it means pain, suffering, loneliness and sorrow. If you transgress now, you will add to the weight of sorrow endured by the Aeon as it hangs on the Elemental Cross[15] – NOT the Calvary Cross[16] please note, but the cross of the elements that make up human existence. *What is more, you will know this.* So now you must weigh your words, thoughts, deeds and actions carefully. Imagine it is someone you love on that elemental cross and that everything you did or said that was wrong caused them more pain.

Do you still think being an initiate is fun!!

What does the Second Degree offer?

It offers harmony, a balance within yourself, with your school and in your approach to the Mysteries. Above all it harmonises your relationship with your higher self. In some systems this makes you Adeptus Minores (see Appendix). The finer tuning of the seed means that you will be able to receive and understand more from the Master of your school. You will be able to achieve a stronger rapport with the Contact. You may find yourself waking up in the small hours with ideas you have to write down. It is indeed a time when many initiates begin to think in terms of writing books, lecturing and taking on some of the teaching burdens from the head of their school.

It is also a time when, if it has not already happened, you may think of setting up a lodge within your school. You are becoming a teacher in your own right.

The balance within the heart centre is adjusting. Often after a period of time you may be beset by problems, or faced with a major change, even an upheaval in your physical life. This is part of the adjustment; there may be something in your life that needs to be qualified before you go further. Address it using the harmony that has been given to you by the seed.

It is at this point that you really begin to understand that the seed is the hologrammatic image of the MASTER behind the school. It contains the wisdom, patience, love and understanding of this Lord of Light. If you allow it to do so, it will help you. It will not always help you, some things you have to do by yourself. Sometimes the seed may seem inactive. This is merely because it has been decided that this is a time for you to be alone.

This may cause waves of loneliness and a feeling of being abandoned. I tell you this from personal experience, *you will never be alone*. You may not see it, feel or hear the seed, but it is there. This is as close to being indwelt as 90% of human beings will get. It is enough, believe me; full indwelling is a weight hard to bear.

The loneliness is caused by the fact that you have irrevocably stepped outside your life wave. You are now a servant of the Lords of Light, who in turn serve humanity. You can only serve if you step back from what is being served. To *serve* you must *observe*. You can only do this well if you place distance between you. You have become a Watcher. You will find yourself observing those around you. At first you will judge them; this is a natural thing and you won't be able to help it. But gradually you will be able to look without judging and then you will know for sure that your own internal scales will have balanced and your heart will have been weighed.

What does this degree ask of the initiate?

Knowledge. It asks that you gather knowledge and disseminate it among those you serve. All initiates are teachers in one sense or another. It is now your task to find even just one person to whom you can pass on your knowledge: all that you have found out, tested, experienced and know to be true.

In SOL the symbol of the First Degree is the bee who serves the hive and works for the good of the whole. The initiate desires to serve and to that end seeks to know the world around him.

The symbol of the Second Degree is the wheatsheaf, the heavy-eared ripe corn that is gathered and bound ready to feed the hungry. In this case those around you are hungry for knowledge. Grind the corn of your experience and from it make the bread with which to feed them.

What happens if a Second Degree initiation goes wrong?

This is far more serious than when it happens to a First Degree. It cannot be revoked; the initiate will go through the tests and hurdles destined. If they have doubts they should have spoken and asked for a delay. If their confusion is genuine they may be gently pressured towards something more suited to their way of thinking, but even so they will be tested.

If a Second Degree is offered and accepted but with a hidden agenda the seed itself will react. Normally a seed lies quiet and exists in harmony with its host. If there has been a disregard for truth or for the Master Contact, the seed may become the instrument by which balance is enforced by whatever means necessary.

The Chosen Road

By Stephanie

"It was extremely clear to me, irrevocably so, that my life is tied to working in the Mysteries and that's my purpose for being here."

When Paul voiced this realisation to me, it was two years practically to the day that he had been initiated into the Second Degree; a period during which he was spurred on to do a number of things that in retrospect may be seen to be laying the foundation for a new magical school.

In May 2003 he changed the name of a prototype company he had set up to reflect its new focus on training in personal development and the magical arts. Then in March 2004 he completed a thesis for a PHD in esoteric science called *Training in the Western Mystery Tradition: A 21st Century Approach* and the following November he gave a talk on it at the annual gathering of SOL lodges.

Paul called this talk *The New Hermetics[17]*, which he says:

"is not really any different from what we did before, it's simply using different language to express how it works in perhaps more scientific ways; it also represents to a degree a coming together of the psychological and the magical in a way that Jung probably would have much appreciated; and it's giving (people) a practical basis for understanding what they're doing."

The New Hermetics

It is a basic premise of Paul's thesis that emotional and mental development need to accompany spiritual development in order for students of the esoteric 'properly to integrate magic...into their daily lives and (so) enhance the quality of their lives and relationships'. 'Without emotional and mental development,' he goes on to say, 'there is the ever present danger that the conscious mind can become over-inflated with the sense of personal power and psychic abilities that are often awakened by esoteric training.'

In this Paul is not saying anything so very different from Dion Fortune, who described herself as 'one of the earliest students of psychoanalysis'[18] and Israel Regardie, who wrote of 'the tremendous value and importance of psychotherapy as a prelude to any serious magical training'[19].

Paul also advocates teaching magic 'from another level which we wouldn't have had to do in the past':-

> *"This is to my mind the key difference between say the way the Golden Dawn[20] worked at the beginning of the 20th century and the way that what we do now should work at the beginning of the 21st century. We should be teaching people also everything from a meta level: in other words how what they are doing works and why it works."*

Paul cites as an example the use of ritual, which he describes as 'not just a beautiful sacred art form in itself':

> *"We also have to explain to them why, so you're creating a different physical context, it's an ability to shift consciousness; that the incense and the stuff are used because they affect the limbic system, because they allow you to access deep memory, because they allow you to easily shift out of mundane into altered states of consciousness – we have to do both, so people see the value of it and understand how it works."*

Let us now pick up the thread of the Uranus and Neptune transits that we have been following throughout Paul's story. From April 2002 to December 2003 Uranus was opposing its own place in Paul's chart, while from March 2003 to January 2005 Neptune was squaring its own place. The Uranus opposition and the Neptune square, as they are known, are two of the key transits that we all experience as we enter the middle years of life, a time when we tend to look within and to the spiritual after having generally spent the early years largely in the external world, building a career and having a family. For Paul though, these transits – with Uranus ruling all his planets in Aquarius (and opposing his Sun Jupiter) and Neptune squaring the cluster in the early degrees of this sign, as well as the South Node – have been a massive 'double whammy'.

I have focused on Uranus and Neptune but of course there were other things going on too: in particular Saturn's transit through fellow Air sign, Gemini reaching the degree of Paul's Midheaven – a career peak – in May 2003 (the month he changed the name of his company and two months after he had been initiated into the Second Degree). Pluto was also bearing down on this point from the opposite sign of Sagittarius, intimating that Paul's life was slowly but inexorably going in a new direction.

But back to Uranus. In March 2003 the planet of change and innovation entered Pisces and from then on right up until January 2005 was periodically in trine to Paul's Moon in early Cancer. It was just after Uranus had aspected his Moon for the fourth and final time that Paul's lodge was raised. Interestingly, the transiting Moon was also in Cancer, just as it had been on the occasion of the consecration of Paul's temple; when he took his oath, as Officer of the East and Magus, it was within less than half a degree's orb.

Later that year, in December 2005, Paul would be initiated into the Third Degree. But first let's see where Erica had got to on the chosen road.

'I have an increased desire to serve'

One year after she had been initiated into the Second Degree Erica's new lodge was also raised, in response to an email from Dolores first mooting the idea in early 2005. It's interesting to note here that Saturn entered Leo in July of that year and the story of its transit through that sign is the story of how Erica came into her North Node as a leader and magus.

> *"I wonder how many new magi balk at such a task being set before them. For some of course it is their desire to set up a new lodge, but others will be asked. For some too, to be a leader or magus will be natural for them; for me it is not, for I am more at home within the silence of my own thoughts. However the experience of stepping out of one's comfort zone is good for one and it is certainly a learning experience. We are here to stretch ourselves and to grow within our current sphere and as my Spirit Friend put it, if the young 'can be confident and can extend themselves in a small container, then they may be suitable for a larger one.'"*

Erica's lodge was raised in November 2005; Saturn had already conjuncted her IC and opposed her MC for the first time and would shortly go retrograde; by the time it had finished toing and froing over these crucial angles, in June 2006, she would have established herself as the magus of a new SOL lodge with strong links to the ancient and sacred isle of Iona, which lies off the island of Mull off the West coast of Scotland.

Iona was made famous by St Columba (*Colum Cille* in Gaelic), who sailed across the sea to it from Ireland in 563 AD with 12 monk companions after a battle over a book, of which he had made a copy that he refused to return. Of such stuff is history made and legends born.

On this tiny island, only three miles long and one mile wide, Columba proceeded to build a church and found a monastery, from which he and his missionary priests evangelised much of pagan Scotland and northern England. Henceforth Iona would be known as the birthplace of Celtic Christianity.

In early August 2007 Erica organised a workshop there, led by Dolores. It was a double first: the first workshop Erica had ever organised and the first time Dolores had ever set foot on the island. By then Saturn had passed over Erica's North Node and in one month's time would leave Leo. Its transit of this sign, ruled by the Sun and associated above all with the self, can be seen almost as a kind of rite of passage for Erica, in which she laid the foundation for a sense of self on which she could build for many years.

A final word on Uranus, which has figured so large in Erica's story. By the time of the workshop on Iona, it had got to within three degrees of her Sun in Pisces, opening her up to a new way of being and the possibility of a new role within the group. Neptune, meanwhile, was within four degrees of her South Node in Aquarius, facilitating the flow of knowledge from the past. 'It is important to me to teach from my own experience,' Erica wrote me, 'I have an increased desire to serve'.

Far down the path

The Second Degree has taken us far down the path. From here the First, which seemed so big at the time, may seem a long way away. This is not to detract from the First – the first of anything is big: the first kiss, the first time you fall in love, your first child, your first book. But to get as far as the Second, to pass the tests it puts in your way, to answer the call to gather up your knowledge, wisdom and experience and disseminate it among those eager and hungry to learn – you will have to screw your courage to the sticking point, hone your will and open your heart to the fullest of which it's capable.

The tests get tougher the further you advance – all part of the process that Dolores describes in her introduction as 'polishing' by the Lords of Light in order to help us to evolve into higher, more spiritual beings. But the rewards are commensurately greater, too: the booklets Erica started producing after she had been initiated into the Second Degree – of which there are now seven at the time of writing – are full of wisdom, both garnered and mediated; while Paul, as we have seen, put a number of important building blocks in place for the new magical school he hoped to found.

But please note that the gifts called upon here, either existing or latent, must be put to use in the service of your fellow human beings in some way. At the Second the call to serve is greater than at the First.

It is even greater at the Third.

THE THIRD DEGREE

The Candidates

By Stephanie

"It was like my covenant, my promise or my pledge – you know, what I promised to myself and to those Others, and that was not actually a difficult thing for me. I will not deviate from that, no matter what my life circumstances are, that is always what I will be doing."

I had no sooner started work on the Third, the most senior degree that SOL confers, than I ran into difficulties. I had to rethink and restructure the book, bolstered in no small part by Dolores, who twice came to the phone in the middle of a busy transatlantic tour to speak to me. What was going on?

An image came to mind of various beings, too shadowy for me to make out their 'faces', putting their heads above the parapet – showing themselves to me, in other words, but not fully – in order to say, So you want to write about the Third, do you? Just who do you think you are?. I quailed before them, but a small logical voice inside me pointed out that I could hardly write about the First and Second Degrees without writing about the Third. The heads disappeared, but they left an impression on me that I did not forget.

It reminded me of what one interviewee, describing the aftermath of her own Third Degree initiation in an email to me, called 'the chaos that seems to follow a Third Degree initiation'. Having supported a friend through his Third Degree initiation, I would expand on that by saying, the chaos that seems to *surround* a Third Degree initiation, i.e., that manifests in the life before, during and after the taking of this critical degree.

It would be wrong of Dolores or myself to give the impression that one progresses automatically from First to Second to Third. It simply doesn't work like that. In part two of this chapter, *The Violet Cord*, Dolores speaks of the 'very careful selection' of candidates for the Third. At the time of writing there are less than two dozen men and women who have been initiated into the Third Degree of the Servants of the Light. Now, SOL has had thousands of students in the 30 and more years that it has been going, which gives you some idea of how rarely this degree is awarded. Among the responsibilities it confers is passing the teaching on and initiating those deemed worthy and ready into the First Degree. The Third calls for nothing less than total, or unreserved, dedication.

What kind of person makes this vow? What kind of person is prepared to juggle service to the Light with the commitments of family, job and the demands of the material world?

I spoke to several people who had made the Unreserved Dedication, among them Ariane, whom we shall feature as the case study for this chapter and Paul, whom we met in the previous chapter on the Second Degree. They all spoke of 'knowing' well in advance that they would be initiated into the Third Degree: one dreamed about receiving a letter with an invitation to take it; Paul had another intense encounter with the Opener on the astral; and 'a feeling came over' Ariane as Dolores was tying the silver cord around her waist that she was going to get the Third.

In fact Ariane had had an intimation even before then that she would be initiated into the Third Degree. "When I was about to receive my Second Degree initiation, I had to go out and buy slippers and I was at this large department store and they happened to have a pair of lavender slippers there at the same time and this little voice said, well you might as well just buy them too! And I was going, God – stop it, stop it! Just – no – go away – I'm just buying these blue ones and – begone." Subsequently Ariane was indeed offered the Third Degree and went back to the department store, this time to buy a pair of lavender slippers. Sorting through the sale racks she found right at the back a pair that happened to be in her size, 'just sitting there waiting for me.'

Just over two years had elapsed between Ariane taking the Second and Third Degrees – two years in which she was in effect in the run-up to her

Third. So what, I asked her, was that period like, in both a magical and a mundane sense?

> *"I was drawn into doing some teaching of ritual magic...I was being really thrust into situations that I probably would have held back on, myself, and so I was very challenged on a personal level...just in a sense of feeling that I was capable, that I was worthy, that I could actually do what was being asked of me and do it well.*

> *"There's kind of a double edge to that in that it was also very exciting and very much what I wanted to do...it felt like my life's blood, but there was a part of me that at the same time felt somewhat inadequate, uncertain and that sort of thing."*

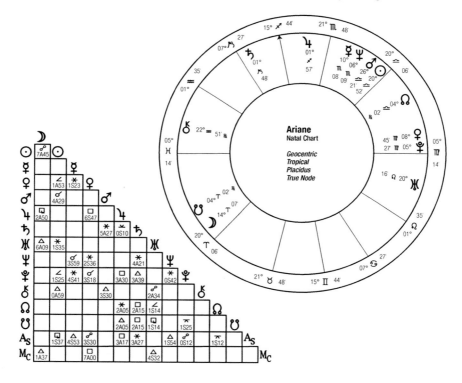

Fig 13

The conflict that Ariane describes between rising to the challenge of teaching magic and questioning her ability to do so, her excitement and feelings of self-doubt, is exactly mirrored in her natal chart (*fig 13*). Ariane has a strong, confident Sun and Mars in Libra and Moon in fiery, Mars-ruled Aries, but her Ascendant is in sensitive Pisces, ruled by Neptune which is situated only 10 degrees from Mars. The Moon's Nodes also lie across the Aries Libra axis and are squared by Saturn, strong in its own sign, Capricorn and in its own house, the 10th. The whole configuration describes someone who's driven to succeed and who dares to do things that other people might balk at but who, in her own words, 'suffers somewhat through them!"

Ariane also published a book during the run-up to her Third and ran a lodge with Rowan, a partnership that she describes as having played an important part in her magical life. I mention this because, as we have seen, Ariane has both masculine planets, the Sun and Mars in the relationship sign of Libra in the eighth house of relationships. Her North Node is also in Libra in the other relationship house, the seventh. So male partners in particular, from her husband to her co-magus to her therapist (whom we shall meet in Part Three of this chapter) are instrumental in helping Ariane to fulfil the work she has incarnated to do.

There were also mundane pressures on Ariane in the two years before she took the Third. As well as bringing up two children, she trained to become a psychotherapist. "There were just a lot of pressures. I probably didn't sleep for two years! There was an extraordinary amount of stress."

Knowing how important keeping things in balance is to Librans and knowing also how magic has a tendency to take over one's life, I asked Ariane if in any sense she had had to choose the magical over the mundane.

> *"In a sense I did and for me how that manifested was about having it OK that people knew about my magical life – I mean, I'm a pretty traditional psychotherapist: I don't employ any wayout practices in my work with people; I'm pretty just run-of-the-mill…and it had to be kind of OK for me first of all when the book was published – I mean, to have clients look me up on the internet and find out that I've written this book or that I'm associated with SOL and there was a decision at some point around me needing to be OK that this be public."*

It was important to Ariane not only that she keep the magical and mundane aspects of her life going simultaneously, but also *harmoniously* (another key Libran word). "It's very important that one doesn't take over the other and I can keep both in balance and they can live side by side but not necessarily in each other's house. I mean there might be doorways between the two…"

In Part Three we shall see that this question of maintaining a balance between the mundane and the magical is something that Paul, also married with children, regards as the biggest challenge facing him. "How do I make it all fit together: family, work, marriage, magic, the lot. I actually feel that a really big challenge…I think it's different, quite honestly, if you're not married or even if you don't have kids."

Guarded secret

In the next section of this chapter, *The Violet Cord*, Dolores refers to the actual initiation into the Third Degree as 'a guarded secret'. In an interview I recorded with her in August 2004 for the members only section of the SOL website she was a little more forthcoming. I asked her what had been the most memorable initiation she had ever conducted. She thought for a long moment and then said that it would have to be Jorge's Third Degree. Jorge is Mexican and the first person Dolores initiated into the Third Degree in the year 2000.

> *"It was like watching somebody go through 12 hours of growth. I mean, people look at me and say, it takes 12 hours? And I say yes: it takes 12 hours. I usually start at 12 noon and the final initiation is at midnight. Of course they have somebody with them every step of the way, but that person can't talk to them and they don't know what the initiate must do. They take in an envelope and the instructions are in there. The initiate does not know, has no idea what they are going to be asked to do. It's wonderful when they come out – I mean, in Jorge's last hour, he* shone*, he really did."*

Dolores counts Jorge 'a great success'. "His life totally belongs to this kind of work now. He's done so much and he's got his own school, his own group, his own order and he's writing books – it's wonderful to see."

Jorge heads up the Fraternidad del Circulo Dorado (Fraternity of the Golden Circle) which has been going for some 20 years. The school's motto is 'Sigue la Luz, no la Lampara' which means, 'Follow the Light not the Lamp'. It has developed a magical training system that offers weekly lessons in Spanish on occult philosophy, the Mystical Qabalah, Tarot and ritual magic. Currently it has students in Mexico, the US, Spain and throughout South America. Jorge himself has written five books on the Hebrew letters, Qabalistic angelic magic, esoteric astrology and the Tarot. "Dolores has been a brilliant light in my life," Jorge wrote me, "without her I wouldn't have been able to accomplish so many things."

So what's it like to go through a Third Degree initiation? I had to ask, even although I knew I would receive the most guarded of all the answers to my questions about the Third. "I don't know how much I'm allowed to say," said one Third I spoke to, startled. "It's – it's – you go through a whole range of – I mean, to say emotions is not even touching – … Yes, you are on your own… you are very much on your own and at the end, in the final hour, Dolores is saying, OK: here is your magical ring, here is your magical cord for this degree – well, you're the priest, you sort it! It's very much kind of you assuming your priesthood."

"It was certainly to start with," said Paul, "a really nerve-wracking experience 'cause you hadn't a clue what you were going to be let in for, but I think once it started and you kind of got into the swing of it, then it was actually a really enjoyable experience."

Ariane told me that she felt tested physically and challenged both emotionally and magically. Then she said something that made me prick up my ears.

Ariane: For me the experience that started there, and then continued afterwards was very much of a death experience.

SVN: Did you say 'death' – d-e-a-t-h?

Ariane: Yes – death.

SVN: In what sense?

Ariane: In the sense that I was leaving a life that I knew and I was entering into a very different life where I may still have connections with that life that I previously had, but my purpose and my activities were different. It's difficult to describe without saying stuff that I actually don't want to talk about… It was just very clear, a very clear demarcation very early on in the initiation that this is what it was about, at least for me.

SVN: Was there a sense of having arrived on the other side of the abyss? Because when you said 'death' the word that came into my mind was 'daath'[21] (there is after all only one letter difference). Was it an 'abyss' experience for you?

Ariane: Well, it was probably two years of being *in* the abyss –

SVN: What – you mean before you got there?

Ariane: Yeah...before I actually touched on some semblance of solid ground. So I wouldn't say that I had had the experience of actually reaching the other side, it was more the experience of going into something and knowing I was leaving something very familiar; going into something more unfamiliar...

With four planets in the eighth house, two of them in Scorpio, Ariane is naturally attuned to the process of death, regeneration and rebirth associated with both this house and sign. She told me that during the initiation some of the inner places she had been to 'were very much symbolically related to death, and oddly it was comforting at the time!'.

She explained what she meant.

"I did not feel alone. I felt like there was a lot of midwives around me and I'm speaking on the inner – there were midwives on the outer too – but there was this sense of midwives on the inner and I was being well cared for, so it was comforting in that way."

Fig 14

A look at the synastry between Ariane and the start of her Third Degree initiation, shown on the biwheel in *fig 14*, with her natal planets on the inside and the planets for the start of the initiation on the outside, gives an astrological insight into what was going on. The first thing to be said is that the entire ritual was held in the dark of the Moon, which was in Scorpio from beginning to end. At the start the Moon, which is of course associated with the feminine, was applying to Ariane's Mercury and Neptune (the planet that rules her chart); by the end it had separated from them. This alone immediately conjures up a picture of women working quietly and intensely – and unseen – to effect a birth. I asked Ariane if any men had been present at her initiation. No, she said, they had all been women. Astrology is nothing if not sometimes stunningly literal.

The other thing to notice is that Ariane's initiation was held on a station of Uranus: on that very day, the planet of the sudden and unexpected positioned itself to go forwards, having been travelling backwards for the last six months. It was at three degrees of Pisces, only two degrees off Ariane's Ascendant. "I certainly didn't expect the reaction I had afterwards, the next day and the days after I felt so separate, alone. Like I said, during the initiation I felt midwived and comforted and not alone and suddenly it just felt like the umbilical cord had been cut and I was alone and I was outside in the cold by myself. And that was very difficult – that was very difficult."

Only three days earlier Saturn had also stationed, in Cancer, which is ruled by the Moon, square, or at right angles, to Ariane's eighth house Sun and Mars in Libra. This describes her experience of being physically and emotionally challenged, as well as tested on her knowledge of magic.

These two key stations of Saturn and Uranus indicate that Ariane's Third Degree initiation was indeed the vehicle by means of which she would leave one life behind, in order to embark on another. When I interviewed her two years on and invited her to look back at it, she said, "It felt like a stripping, I was just being stripped bare".

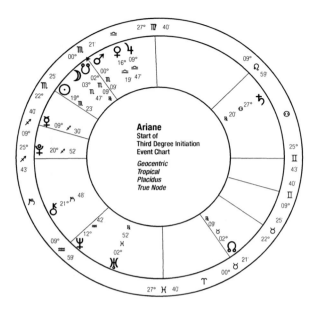

Fig 15

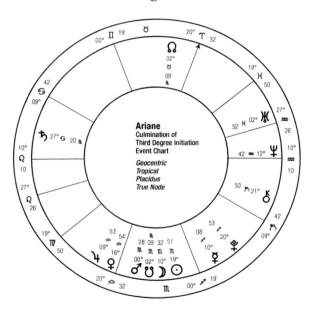

Fig 16

The charts for the start and culmination of Ariane's Third Degree initiation (*figs 15 and 16*) show in the first instance planets bunched around the Midheaven and in the second at the bottom, or nadir, of the chart. Ariane confirmed that what had started out as an external or outer experience culminated in an intense internal experience. This is how another Third described it:-

> "It started off feeling like this is just a recognition of what you've been through over the last 12 hours and that in a sense is a microcosm of what you've been through in your lives before this, but again, there is a very definite conferring of...something, and I explained to Dolores afterwards how it felt. It was like there was a funnel of light behind her and it poured down through her and into me, and it was like this sort of golden person – person is such an inadequate word – was pushing this through her and into me, and I assumed, I took on something – almost a mantle, an overshadowing...".

The whole 12 hours of the Third Degree initiation ritual builds up to this point with the pressure increasing hour by hour, as is evident from this entry that Paul wrote in his magical journal at the ninth hour.

> "I'm humbled by the trust that the inner plane beings have placed in me, so what does this mean for me now at the ninth hour of the ritual? It means that for the first time I know how far I have come. I'm beginning to understand the responsibilities being placed upon me. I acknowledge those other Third Degrees who have similarly been accepted by the angelic realms. I can see the thread through my life that has brought me to this point. I know that in order to command the respect and obedience of the inner plane guardians I have promised to uphold and teach the light of the Mysteries. This is why the inner plane guardians have placed their trust in me. So I now have something to live up to which I had not committed to before commencing this rite. To put it crudely, in some ways it's a quid pro quo in that in return for the respect and the obedience of the inner plane guardians I commit my life to teaching the Mysteries. I more fully understand that now and it's OK. It hasn't changed my commitment to go on, or my decision to commit my life to the Lords of Light. It's still a somewhat scary thought but it doesn't change it. At this point I know I will make the Unreserved Dedication and I'm pondering the form of words I will use for it."

That was the last thing Paul wrote before he made the Unreserved Dedication.

The Unreserved Dedication

In the interview I recorded with Dolores she speaks of the initiate, when it comes to the Third Degree, having to make 'a great choice' and likens it to Jesus going into the Garden of Gethsemane[22]. "You could say He was approaching, on a cosmic scale, His Third Degree initiation. He had a choice; He was saying, let this cup pass from me – I don't want to do it! But He did, in the end, and the Third Degree is when you accept that you have to be, in one sense, a saviour."

"For me I don't feel like I have a choice," said Ariane, when I put this to her, " because I feel like it's kind of hard-wired into me... like it's kind of, y'know, in my DNA...".

"There is just this sense," said another Third, after a thinking pause that lasted eight seconds, "that I've dedicated myself to the Lords of Light and that's it, really – what do you want me to do?"

"The Unreserved Dedication for me," Paul said, "isn't about a personal commitment to a person or a thing, it's about a commitment to bringing other people to their own light."

The Third is a torch-bearer, of the Light that must be carried on from one generation to the next, in order that it not be lost and the Dark prevail. So what is this Light that they all must serve? It is, as Dolores says in The Violet Cord, 'the flame of knowledge, service and dedication'. The initiate who makes the Unreserved Dedication commits to taking up the torch and passing it on in his or her turn. The more initiates there are to do this, the further the Light will spread, until such time as all humanity is brought within its circle.

"It was like I was very clear about what I can offer," said Ariane, "not necessarily who I offer it to or how I offer it, but my commitment, what binds me to the Work and I was also given some inner direction around that as well. It was like my covenant, my promise or my pledge – you know, what I promised to myself and to those Others, and that was not actually a difficult thing for me. I will not deviate from that, no matter what my life circumstances are, that is always what I will be doing."

For Ariane a large part of this is teaching, as it is for Paul.

"I see it as a commitment to the teaching and perpetuation of the Mysteries. Now for me that is about the Western Mystery tradition specifically, so the question arises why would we want to do that? For me it's about empowering other people to become the best they can be and I don't mean that in a kind of Anthony Robbins[23] sense; I mean it in a sense of being spiritually evolved. By the way I don't see the Third Degree as being a badge of spiritual evolution for people; I see it as an acknowledgment of the work someone's done, but I see it much more as an acknowledgment of them making the Unreserved Dedication, and for me that's what the Third Degree's all about."

Reading the transcripts of all the interviews I had recorded for this chapter sent me in search of the Introduction to the SOL course. At the bottom of page 10 I found what I was looking for. This is what Dolores wrote around 30 years ago, after she had taken over SOL from its founder, W.E. Butler:-

"To TEACH, that is our aim. To teach well, and with love. To teach what we have been taught; and in that teaching to form close-knit bonds that will bring all faiths and traditions into one united brotherhood. The SOL is pendant to the ancient school of Alexandria, where all faiths and beliefs were welcomed and their knowledge shared. We do NOT teach any faith or religion, or exalt any one above another. Though we teach the Western Way, we do not oppose that of the East; but look upon it as one of the many bright strands of faith that make up the Divine Pattern."

Although these words were written in another century, indeed in another millennium, I was struck by how Aquarian they sounded. A fitting mission statement, it seemed to me, for a school whose initiates must light the way for others to follow into the Age of Aquarius.

The Violet Cord

By Dolores

Cord Colours and the Houses

In the school of the Servants of the Light we have five different cord colours. Students working on the foundation and main courses up to lesson 12 wear a white cord over a black robe or cassock. On completing lesson 12 they may apply for and wear a golden cord. Once they have attended all three in the series of ritual magic training workshops they may put either three blue wooden beads on this cord or tie three knots into it.

The golden cord changes to red at the first initiation, then to silver at the second; the third cord is violet. The First Degree is linked to the Fraternitatus Alexandrae, the second to the House of Light and the third to the House of the Amethyst. This is a fairly typical arrangement that has similarities with many other schools and orders.

In the SOL a First Degree initiate follows the path of the Bee, in that they serve in ways best suited to their talents and the time they can spare from work and families. A Second Degree initiate walks the path of the Wheat Sheaf, a gatherer of knowledge, often a supervisor or a compiler of information; again according to the time they have to spare from their everyday life, they are often either an officer in a working lodge or may head such a lodge. A Third Degree initiate treads the path of the Lamp. In effect they become that which encloses the flame of knowledge, service and dedication. The flame itself is the Inner Plane Master behind the school.

Is the source of power the same as for the First and Second Degrees?

Yes, it is further tuned and refined to match the growing abilities of the initiate and to enable them to cope with the new demands upon their time and energies that they now have to meet. From now on their lives will be divided between the everyday world and the spiritual. Up to this point they can withdraw at any time, in fact they could still do that, but with greater cost to their spiritual advancement. This is the reason for the very careful selection of candidates for the Third Degree. The dedication must be as deep as they are able to offer. It is preferable that their families are grown and therefore not as needful of their presence and guidance, or that they are an adult partnership where no children are involved. The SOL tries not to overload supervisors who have young families and is mindful that partners who may not be involved with the school are to be considered at all times. However sometimes a candidate is so obviously ready for the next step that it cannot be denied.

What new demands does a Third Degree place upon the candidate?

To begin with a Third may initiate a candidate to the First Degree, on the approval of the head of the school. They may after a further time and at the discretion of the Head, be given permission to initiate to the Second Degree. They must learn to observe and judge the capabilities of those around them, in their lodge or under their supervision. They will almost certainly be faced with tests concerning those in their keeping. They may be called upon to take over some of the tasks and duties of the head of school and to deputise for them when it is needed.

It is also a time when their personal contact with the Master Teacher grows deeper and more intense. Among the tests they may face is a growing ego.

It happens at each degree, but at the Third it is far subtler. There is a desire (so they may think) to lift some of the burden from the head of the school, which is commendable, until they suddenly realise that what they are doing is more along the lines of a takeover!

This holds many dangers for both the school and the initiate. A gentle reminder of where the Contact and the power actually lie is often enough to bring about a realisation of what is happening. But if this is not enough a firm word or two…well, maybe three or four, can be administered. There is a recognised syndrome in occult training referred to as 'the Star Pupil

Syndrome': when someone who has been groomed for office decides that their teacher is no longer capable of the work and that he or she, as a Third Degree is, in their own opinion, manifestly more capable of it. This is not confined to Thirds; I have seen it happen with Seconds and even with a First Degree. The thing is they have convinced themselves that they are right.

It can, if not handled right away and with firmness, cause great damage to a lodge and the school to which it is pendant. It is rare, but it happens. The Inner Plane Master will let the head of school know when it is right to hand over to the next generation. Lucky is the head of school who is surrounded by level-headed, dedicated and well-trained initiates of all three degrees.

But in the main, if the training has been good and undertaken with true dedication, a Third Degree initiate can look forward to a gradual flowering of the inner contact with the Master Teacher and a strengthening of their personal psychic talents. They become aware of an increased capacity for love, wisdom and understanding; combined, this is the power of the magician who stands on the threshold of Adeptus Majores (see Appendix).

From now on the task is to prepare to tread the path leading from Geburah to Chesed, the path of the Adeptus Exemptus (see Appendix). It will of course lead to the inevitable test and here it is faith that is tested. It is the darkest of the dark nights of the soul.

From personal experience I can tell you that the moment when you, *seemingly*, lose your faith in all that you have worked for, trained for and dedicated yourself to, is the most devastating test of all. I can also tell you, though you will not believe it when it happens, that you will never be left alone, that the faith you think is lost is still there. What is left to you is the determination not to be overcome.

This is the moment to cling to the symbol of the Third Degree, the Lamp with the asbestos wick. The Lamp is your physical self, the weakest part of you, the wick is your higher self and the flame surrounding the wick is the test you are undergoing. The Lords of Flame are using their own Light to burn away the last vestiges of dross from your spirit. *As the asbestos wick, you cannot be consumed.* Believe in that and you will come through.

What takes place in a Third Degree initiation?

It differs greatly from school to school and the ceremony itself is a guarded secret. Suffice to say that it will last for many hours and you will need every bit of knowledge you have gathered over the years, some of which you may even have forgotten. You will be isolated, but watched over, alone and not alone, seen but ignored. It will exhaust you, test you and demand from you. It will provide you with knowledge that will be yours alone, and forever.

At the end of it you will wear the violet robe and the slippers that will carry you over the crystal bridge spanning the Abyss, the violet cord of your rank, and the ring of the adept. These of course pertain to the SOL, but it will be fairly similar to most Contacted schools.

Tuning the Seed to the Third Degree

If you were to look inside an ordinary seed of a flower or tree you would find at its very core the minute point of life that holds the potential of its final form. When you receive the seed of initiation at the First Degree, that tiny point lies within it. What you may not realise is that this is a spark that will grow into a flame if allowed and encouraged to do so.

At the Second Degree it awakens and glows. When you come before your earthly teacher at the Third Degree, the seed within the teacher flames into a spiritual fire and is passed to you and into the seed within you sparking it into flame. This becomes the inner light that will now mark you for the rest of your life.

At the giving of the red cord, the sigil of the School was placed into your aura at the head. With the giving of the silver cord the sigil became visible to spiritual sight in your heart centre. Now it is placed into the sacral centre, where the point of God, your inheritance from The One is housed. Where else would one find the incredible gift of creative power from a supreme Creator? You are now awakened from head to toe. Your creative gifts are yours to use in the way your talents lie. You are whole.

What does all this mean?

You had responsibility and then you gave it back. Now you take it on again but with a greater knowledge of what it entails. With this degree and for the rest of this incarnation you lift the weight of one human soul from the Aeon of the Age. One thorn from the crown you might say. You are in effect sharing the suffering of the Aeon simply by understanding who and what you are and what the Aeon actually is.

Does a Third Degree ever go wrong?

Anything can go wrong if you work at it! Yes it can go wrong, it does not happen often because if you reach that point in your training and knowledge you are also well aware of the consequences. Sometimes the whole thing overwhelms you and you can close down spiritually in a reaction to what is going on inside you. Think of it as being rather like a spiritual coma. You may come out of it and recover your spiritual senses, or you may hover in a twilight zone where everything is like a dream that is never going to be realised. Sometimes it needs a shock to awaken it again. The best way to avoid any of this is to make quite certain you know what you are doing if you accept a Third Degree.

Each degree is a new birth for the soul; that means an astrological chart calculated for it can act like a map to guide you through the choppy waters of what comes after the initiation. It can point out your strengths and weaknesses, it often dovetails in an amazing way with your natal chart and your other initiations.

It is worth considering dates if it is at all possible when arranging the initiation time. One can use the knowledge of an expert to make use of the planets and their phases to gain an advantage. That will help rather than hinder. However if such a possibility is not available to you, then mark the time, date and place and the time when the seed is given, or tuned.

The whole reason for this book is that up until now there has been nothing about the importance of these moments in time when you are spiritually at a crossroads in your life. A natal chart is important, so are those moments when eclipses and transits occur. How much more important to know what the planets can tell you when you are standing before an adept and preparing to take a step that will set you apart from your fellow human beings for the rest of your life. A step that will enable you to serve them more deeply than you could by being close to them.

This introduces a whole new application of astrology and one that will I believe become a well-defined tool in magical training of the future. As you will see from the charts and interpretations in this book this is not a flash-in-the-pan idea. It has been carefully researched, thought out and tested.

The most important events in our lives do not happen by accident, there is a time that is right for everything, it will happen when it must. It may be a good time and great things may come of it. It may be a bad time and therefore you will learn valuable lessons from it. The bad times are learning times, they are in fact the only learning times. Good times are great and we enjoy them, but we do not learn from them. They are holidays from the school of life. Life, like school, has regular exams we must all take, and these are the learning times. Initiation increases our ability to deal with them.

Pass or fail, those are our choices.

The Chosen Road

By Stephanie

"I remember coming home and sitting down at my desk and being flooded with ideas for books. I wrote them all down and was completely overwhelmed."

"The lodge work went up a notch, the ability to connect to the inner is greater than it's been before and the connection to the Opener Himself is deeper than it was before."

It can take a while for the effects of initiation to work through. How long that 'while' is varies from individual to individual, depending on their psychic make-up and material circumstances. Some effects may be felt immediately, others not for a year or two. You light the fire, but it takes a while for its warmth to penetrate all four corners of a room.

17 months after she had been initiated into the Third Degree, Ariane emailed me to say that 'the chaos' that seems to follow it had started to abate. "It was kind of like a tidal wave that passed through just about every aspect of my life," she wrote. "However now (hopefully) on the other side, it seems to have been a cleansing and reordering sort of experience."

Ariane told me that her psychotherapy practice had as good as died; at the same time there were difficulties at home that put her marriage under stress. "My husband and I had to make new kind of agreements and arrangements around how we are married. And that was very difficult for me. I had to do a lot of quick footwork and I had to stay calm and do some hard inner work, so I didn't just blow things."

Would it have been easy to blow things, I asked. "Yeah – yeah. It would have been," Ariane said.

"There's pitfalls all over the place", she went on, "I think glamour's one of them, which in Jungian terms is kind of this getting inflated, having a greater sense of oneself than there is and likewise becoming kind of enamoured or bewitched by the magical stuff."

So what techniques does Ariane use to keep the ego from developing too great a sense of its own importance? "Hm," she said, and paused. Then, "I clean my own house" – "Grounding," I said, "nothing like it." "There's nothing like it," Ariane agreed. We laughed, but I couldn't help noticing that Ariane has Venus and Pluto together in Virgo, favoured by Saturn in Capricorn, all in sensible Earth signs. She continued, "I try not to look too far ahead and do what's just in front of me, pay attention to my kids, pay attention to my husband… So I don't know exactly how I do it and I always feel I'm just at as much risk as anybody else for kind of blowing it."

"I don't care how prepared you are for the Third," said Paul, when I interviewed him for this chapter not quite a year on from his own Third Degree initiation, "things are going to get thrown up, for realignment.

"I do feel, and I have to say," he went on, "looking back on this year, it seems like the whole year is a long dark night of the soul. There was a period of calm after the storm, so to speak, in the first three months and then after that things just have been thrown completely up in the air. So whether it's too much work and not enough time to do it in, whether it's trying to keep the relationship with my other half together and make that work, when she's had challenges at work and we have the kids and lots of distractions, it feels like there's an enormous amount of pressure building up."

It was November 2006 and Saturn was moving slowly but inexorably towards its station in early December at 25 degrees Leo, less than one degree off Paul's Sun in Aquarius (*fig 8*). Saturn was halfway through a cycle begun in 1991 when it had entered Aquarius and Paul had started reading Dion Fortune and joined SOL; when it had got up to the degree of his Sun in December 1993, he had gone to one of Dolores' workshops and 'really connected with her'. Paul was approaching a culmination of the magical work he had begun 15 years ago; hence the pressure he now felt to realise his long-held ambition of founding a magical school. By now he already had a name for it, but with Saturn stationing retrograde, he would have to wait until after April 2007, when Saturn started going forwards again on its way out of Leo, to launch it. There was work to do on the inner first.

"So I see less time over time doing the day job, so to speak, because the magical work will start to replace that but also to provide a reasonable amount of money so that's not an issue. And I think that's a challenge – to do it that way and to make it work in the context of family, relationship, work, earning money and creating a magical school. I think that's a different challenge in the 21st century to what many people have had in the 18th, 19th and 20th centuries."

The challenge of balance

With all the Thirds I spoke to I had a sense of the pressure really being on, of it simply not being possible to continue living as they had before, the pull of the magical was too strong. Yet they were married, they had children, jobs – a whole array of mundane responsibilites that they couldn't just abandon. It's what Ariane, with her Moon in Aries opposite her Sun and Mars in Libra, so aptly referred to as the challenge of balance.

In meeting this challenge in her own life, Ariane has had the support of another therapist; like her husband and co-magus, an important male partner for her. "An extraordinarily important partner for me, yeah — in a totally different sense. I've just been very, very fortunate to have found somebody…it was 12/13 years ago…and I've been going to this man ever since and just sharing my dreams and talking about that and whatever else is going on in my life and it has been profoundly helpful."

How, I asked, had it helped her to deal with the stuff that inevitably comes up in a magical training?

"It's helped me to develop myself in a way that I've been able to meet the challenges that have ended up in front of me; it's helped me to work with that challenge of balance, balancing my marriage and trying to remain plain as dirt and just keeping that all going; and for anybody who's considering this path or wants to go further with it, to find that sort of support, whether it's psychotherapy or some other form, you'd be blessed – I feel blessed in that way."

In the chapter on the Second Degree we saw how Paul worked with his training partner to clear the stuff that came up for him before his initiation. In the lead-up to the Third he again worked with her 'to clear emotional stuff and limiting beliefs'.

"Now who knows, if we hadn't done that, what the outcome would have been, 'cause you never know. But my intuitive

feeling is that – there's lots of stuff that comes up – am I capable of doing it, can I make this work and then all the mundane stuff like, I react badly to something my mother or children do, or what my wife says, or something and know that's stuff inside me I need to fix, so I'll go and do it. So if I didn't fix it, what would have happened? My suspicion is that relationships would have got to beyond breaking point. So I think that having those skills allowed me to deal with some of the tensions in the relationships leading up to my Third in a way that at least defused that and got me through a difficult patch."

The Opener

As well as the commitment to teach, initiation into the Third Degree deepens connection to the Inner Plane Master behind SOL, a Contacted school. This is how one of the Thirds I spoke to describes it:

"You recognise, I think, that you're working with the Lords of Light consciously and so much more stuff comes through now, you know – you're sort of sitting, and there's a feeling that you're not alone any more: there's this kind of what becomes an overshadowing; it's almost like a constant presence with you, and everything you do, you think about – what about the implications of this and how will the Lords of Light see that? …You feel much more upheld – I'm on your side and we are working in conscious communion together, so how can we make this happen?"

This Inner Plane Master is commonly referred to within SOL as the Opener, which is short for Opener of the Ways, one of the names by which Anubis, Ancient Egyptian god of the dead, who is usually represented in canine form, is known. Since being initiated into the Third Degree Paul's perception of this Being has shifted, as he explains:

"For me the Opener better describes what that Being or energy pattern does. It is about opening the ways and it is about being a guide and a teacher; it's not about a jackal-headed god of the dead who kind of presides over people being stuffed into mummies – I mean, it's not; it's a different thing completely. Which is why I'm never that comfortable seeing Anubis as a jackal – I'd much rather see Him as the anthropomorphised version, 'cause that's how I see the Opener."

This Being of Light, or energy pattern – it's so difficult to describe in mere words, such a blunt tool with which to give it form; really it can only be experienced, or known in that intuitive sense of 'knowing God' – works through those who are open to it, and can take the energy, and use it to the highest of which they are capable, in different ways, according to their natural talents and abilities. But in each case there is an opening up of psychic channels, that may hitherto have lain fallow, awaiting that moment in an individual incarnation to be seeded anew.

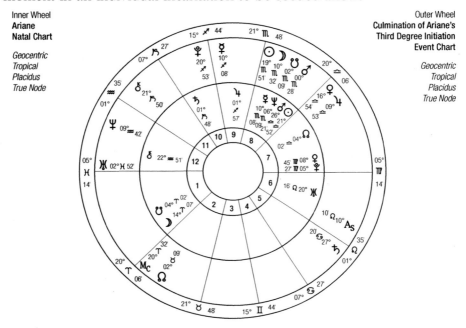

Inner Wheel
Ariane
Natal Chart

Geocentric
Tropical
Placidus
True Node

Outer Wheel
Culmination of Ariane's
Third Degree Initiation
Event Chart

Geocentric
Tropical
Placidus
True Node

Fig 17

In Ariane's case a look at the synastry between her natal chart on the inner wheel and the culmination of her Third Degree initiation ritual on the outer wheel (*fig 17*) shows that all of the latter's planets bar one are situated above the horizon, indicating that the work she has committed to will take her out into the world. Saturn occupies a singular position in the creative fifth house in the bottom half of the chart. At right angles to her Sun and Mars in the eighth house, it will drive Ariane to delve into the Mysteries and to share her understanding of them with others.

By the time I came to interview her, in October 2006, her psychotherapy practice had picked up considerably and she was planning to move to a bigger office, where she could also teach. Then, as I was putting the finishing touches to this chapter, she emailed me to say that her practice had been very busy and she was working on two books 'with a third in the wings and ideas for many more.' "I think that is probably the aftermath of the initiation," she went on. "Whether any of it will get published is another question, but I have enough projects to keep me busy for a lifetime or two. I remember coming home (from my initiation) and sitting down at my desk and being flooded with ideas for books. I wrote them all down and was completely overwhelmed."

Paul, too, experienced an initial surge of psychic energy. "What we noticed in the January February March period after my Third Degree was the lodge rituals went up a notch completely. We were doing Egyptian stuff and we had some very intense lodge ritual experiences on a level never before experienced by the same group of people working together. So I think the lodge work did seriously go up a notch when I got my Third."

Two years down the chosen road Paul elaborated further on the process set in train by his Third Degree initiation:

> "I am certainly more aware of discarnate beings around, especially in ritual. I just have a strong feeling that they're there, and if I focus hard enough I can 'see' them standing around (or crowding in would be a better description) the outside of the circle in which our lodge is working. When I'm writing rituals I often feel more connected... As I write the rituals I can literally hear the people's voices inside my head, and see the ritual unfold in my mind. This is more graphic than it used to be, and has definitely happened since my Third, and wasn't immediate, but has taken a couple of years to manifest."

During that time Paul also put on the first of a series of magical workshops, under the joint auspices of his company and the Servants of the Light – a precursor to a 'next generation' magical school, 'integrating modern personal development techniques with ancient spiritual development practices, with the aim of creating true magicians for the 21st century'.

As a pointer to what lies further down the chosen road for Paul there can be no better example than the mission statement for his school that he wrote specially for this book.

> "Through its quality of teaching, innovation and integrity, we aim to become one of the most respected and influential magical schools of the 21st century.

"We will be known by the quality of our students and graduates, who will demonstrate the highest levels of mental, emotional and spiritual development, and who will integrate this into their everyday lives. They and the school will shine like a beacon, like the Lamp of the Hermit, showing the way for those who would follow."

THE INITIATOR

By Stephanie

Early on in the writing of this book I received a 'mind nudge' that it was to be about not only astrology and initiation, but also Dolores and SOL, the magical school of which she has been Director of Studies and run with her husband, Michael and a dedicated band of supervisors for more than 30 years.

In that time, as well as training thousands of students, giving out the teaching at hundreds of workshops and writing more than 20 books, Dolores has initiated many people to the First, Second and Third Degrees, among them the men and women who have shared their stories for this book. So it seems fitting to end it with a look at her own natal chart and the synastry between that and the chart for her initiation.

I remember the very first time I looked at Dolores' chart. It was in November 1995 and I had just drawn it up. I found myself sitting back at my desk, basking in a wonderful green energy which seemed to rise off the chart, like green sunlight. Dolores is on the green ray; in an email she sent me as I was writing this chapter, she elaborated: 'I began by being pure green, the emerald green of power, but as I grew older and began to learn how to control power, it began to be shaded with the blue and the indigo; just lately the indigo, which is also the mystic ray, has begun to deepen.'

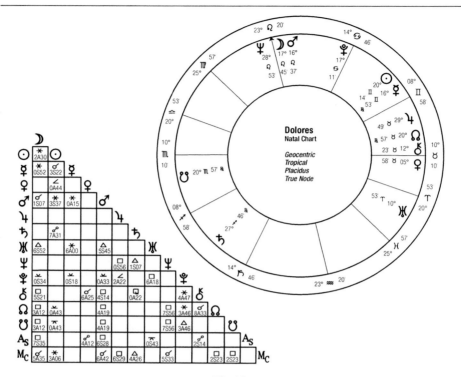

Fig 18

Dolores' birth chart (*fig 18*) is full of power, passion, fire and drama. She has no less than five planets in the Fire signs, including the Moon, Mars – which rules the charismatic Scorpio Ascendant and therefore the chart – and Neptune, all in Leo at the most elevated point. Together with Saturn in Sagittarius and Uranus in Aries they make a triangle, or Grand Trine, of planets in the Fire signs. Fire is positive and believes in itself and its vision for the future.

There is another major pattern in the chart, formed by the South Node in Scorpio lying opposite the North Node, Jupiter, Chiron and Venus in Taurus, all at right angles to the planets in Leo, making a T-square in the fixed signs. The fixed signs are resolute and not easily deterred from the course they set themselves.

The Sun is in Gemini in the eighth house (a common placement, I have found, in the charts of people drawn to the Mysteries), along with its ruler, Mercury; while the ninth house, associated with writing, publishing, study and travel, is emphasised by a stellium of planets, the Moon, Mars and Pluto. This latter planet, incidentally, sits on the midpoint between Dolores' Sun in Gemini and Moon in Leo, at 19 degrees Cancer.

It's a very strong, very powerful chart; the chart of someone who, with the majority of planets above the horizon, cannot fail to make an impact on the world.

Dolores' initation

This is borne out by a look at the chart for Dolores' First Degree initiation (*fig 19*) and the synastry between that and her natal chart (fig 20). Dolores' First is particularly significant because this is when she first made the Unreserved Dedication! "Because I was full of myself and didn't know any better," she told me in an email, "I blew the initiation ritual wide open by giving the Unreserved Dedication at the altar of my initiation!!!!

"The Magus nearly fainted!" she went on. "That was on 8 December 1968" (at the Society of the Inner Light[24] in London).

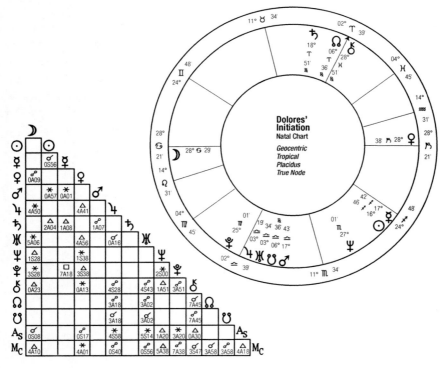

Fig 19

The chart of Dolores' initiation is ruled by the Moon, strong on several counts: it's rising, very closely conjunct the Ascendant; in its own sign, Cancer; and just past Full Moon, which occurred four days previously. As the Moon rises, Venus sets, linking the two feminine planets in a close opposition across the Ascendant Descendant axis. They're further linked by Venus ruling the stellium of planets in Libra in the fourth house, traditionally that of the Moon; in addition, both planets receive many favourable aspects from other planets.

The prominence of these two planets in the chart makes the feminine energy very strong: both the nurturing energy of the Moon and the Venusian energy that makes connections and forms relationships.

The solar, masculine energy is also strong: the Sun's in a Fire sign, in a fiery house, in close aspect to Mars, with both planets aspecting Saturn, which dominates the chart from its natural 10th house of career. Saturn in turn is wide conjunct the North Node: Dolores' task as an initiate lies in the world, where she must give a lead for others to follow.

Perhaps the most striking feature of the chart is that the Moon and Venus, Mars and Saturn form part of a Cardinal Grand Cross, involving no less than six planets in all, as well as the Nodes. This generates a very powerful, dynamic energy: one of the characteristics of the cardinal signs is that they get things moving, they get things off the ground; in other words, they *initiate*. So this is the chart of someone who was initiated to, in turn, initiate others. Dolores is that most powerful of initiates: the initiator.

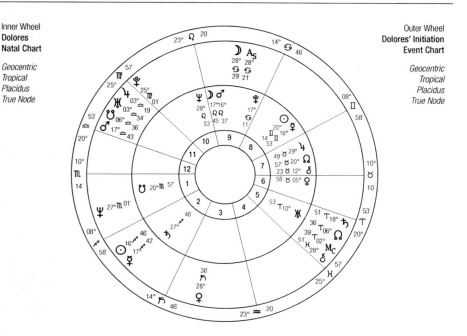

Fig 20

'You have served well'

There are a number of interaspects between Dolores' natal chart (on the inner wheel) and the chart of her initiation (on the outer wheel) (*fig20*) that bring out and strengthen the purpose of the natal chart. The Initiation Sun and Mercury in Sagittarius make a close opposition to the natal Sun and Mercury in Gemini across the second-eighth house axis. Traditionally this axis is associated with the signs of Taurus and Scorpio, in which the natal Nodes fall: the South Node in Scorpio in the first house, the North Node in Taurus in the seventh house, an indication that the work of this incarnation is of a practical nature. The wisdom and power accumulated in a past life or lives must in this life be made manifest and shared with others.

The Initiation Sun and Mercury are also almost exactly trine the natal Moon Mars in Leo, putting Dolores under the spotlight; all that she is and does is for the world to see.

A striking feature of the synastry between the two charts is the number of initiation planets that fall across the fifth-eleventh house axis: Mars, Jupiter and Uranus in Libra in the eleventh; Saturn in Aries in the fifth, together with the North Node. These all fall on the natal Uranus, putting pressure on Dolores to put what she has uniquely to give, out to the collective.

The Initiation Neptune falls on the natal South Node in the first house, in an echo of the natal Neptune in the 10th, which is wide conjunct the Moon and Mars in Leo. Dolores must give of the very essence of herself in the service of others and the initiation acts like a kind of sluice gate, which opens to release the powers dammed up in other lives.

Her task is no less than to bring the Great Work forth, into the public domain, where all who can may benefit from it; the initiation has thrust her into orbit to perform this task and to initiate those who would take the torch from her, so that the Light may burn ever more brightly in the world.

It is to this work that Dolores has given her all, and recently I witnessed her renew the Unreserved Dedication, in a public avowal of a commitment first made 40 years ago. The occasion was a workshop dedicated, appropriately, to the worship of Anubis. In one powerful and moving ritual the earthly form of the God, summoned by the High Priest and High Priestess, appeared and voiced, unprompted, to Dolores the words, 'You have served well'.

A fitting tribute, it seems to me, on which to end this book.

Stephanie V. Norris
June 2008

NOTES

1 Originally the place where members of a local branch of a society met and hence the group itself. In this context a group of people who come together specifically for the purpose of carrying out magical work, usually involving the performing of ritual in a particular esoteric tradition.

2 The inner plane being or discarnate entity that guides and teaches through the initiates of the school.

3 Servants of the Light, a modern-day Western Mystery school teaching the ancient Mysteries by means of correspondence courses, lectures and workshops. Founded in 1972 by W.E. Butler, Dolores and Michael Ashcroft-Nowicki, it has developed into an international organisation teaching the Qabalah, Tarot and Arthurian tradition to thousands of students around the world. Like the Mystery schools of ancient times, the SOL offers this training by means of a three-tier structure, the First, Second and Third Degrees.

4 The Opener of the Ways, one of the names by which Anubis is known.

5 The Western Mysteries, also known as the Western Mystery Tradition or the Western Esoteric Tradition, of which the best known practised today are the Eleusinian or Greek, the Egyptian, Celtic and Qabalistic, as well as those pertaining to the great School of Alexandria and its renowned library.

6 Inscribed on the temple of Apollo at Delphi.

7 Knight, Gareth. *The Secret Tradition in Arthurian Legend*, The Aquarian Press, 1983.

8 The three Rays represent the three paths of love (Violet), wisdom (Blue) and power (Green). Priests with a true vocation always show a violet ray prominent in their auric colours. Teachers tend to have a mixture of blue and green depending upon how and what they teach. Power is the hardest to control. Mixtures of all three can occur as in Ernest Butler and Gareth Knight. Dion Fortune was probably Green Ray with Blue. But the aura has to be 'seen' to know for certain.

9 Time Line Therapy™.

10 *Hamlet* act I sc 3 l 78.

11 Church of England.

12 One of the most famous occult figures of the twentieth century, founder of the Society of the Inner Light and author of *The Mystical Qabalah*, *The Cosmic Doctrine* as well as many occult fiction classics including *Moon Magic* and *The Sea Priestess*.

13 The fae or fairy folk, tiny supernatural beings with magical powers who take an interest in the affairs of humans.

14 W.E. Butler, one of the founders of SOL and Dolores' spiritual mentor.

15 The Elemental Cross has four arms of equal length, representing the four elements, the four winds and the four directions.

16 The Calvary Cross is the cross of the Christian crucifixion with an extended lower limb.

17 The name given to the body of ancient writings and teachings about the occult, alchemy and magic, attributed to Hermes Trismegistus (Hermes Thrice Greatest), associated with Thoth, the Egyptian god of wisdom and Hermes, Greek messenger to the gods.

18 Fortune, Dion. *The Secrets of Doctor Taverner*, Introduction, p9. The Aquarian Press, 1989.

19 Regardie, Israel. *The Middle Pillar*, Introduction to the Second Edition, pviii. Llewellyn Publications, 1978.

20 Hermetic Order of the Golden Dawn, a magical order of the late 19th and early 20th centuries.

21 The sphere on the Tree of Life that is a gateway to other dimensions. The other spheres are Malkuth, Yesod, Hod, Netzach, Tiphereth, Geburah, Chesed, Binah, Chokhmah and Kether. The Western Mystery Tradition uses the Tree of Life for its capacity to hold, explain, unite and expand the multi-patterned universe in which we live.

22 *Mark* 14:36.

23 American life coach, writer and motivational speaker.

24 The Magical order founded by Dion Fortune.

BIBLIOGRAPHY

Ashcroft-Nowicki, Dolores. *The Shining Paths*, Thoth Publications, 1997.

Ashcroft-Nowicki, Dolores. *The New Book of the Dead*, The Aquarian Press, 1992.

Brady, Bernadette. *The Eagle and the Lark*, Samuel Weiser, Inc. 1992.

Crowley, Vivianne. *A Woman's Kabbalah*, Thorsons, 2000.

Fortune, Dion. *The Training & Work of an Initiate*, Samuel Weiser, Inc. 2000

Fortune, Dion. *The Magical Battle of Britain*, Golden Gates Press, 1993.

Hall, Judy. *Patterns of the Past*, The Wessex Astrologer Ltd, 2000.

Huber, Bruno and Louise. *Moon Node Astrology*, HopeWell, 2005

March, Marion D. & McEvers, Joan. *The Only Way to Learn Astrology*, Vol II, Astro Computing Services, 1981.

Norris, Stephanie. *Chiron: Planet of the New Age*, A Thesis for the Diploma of the Centre for Psychological Astrology, 1996.

Regardie, Israel. *The Middle Pillar*, Llewellyn Publications, 1978.

Reinhart, Melanie. *Chiron and the Healing Journey*, Arkana, 1989

Smoley, Richard and Kinney, Jay. *Hidden Wisdom*, Penguin/Arkana, 1999.

Sutcliff, Rosemary. *The Legends of King Arthur*. Part I, *The Sword and the Circle*. Part II, *The Light Beyond the Forest*. Part III, *The Road to Camlann*. Red Fox, 1992.

Tompkins, Sue. *Aspects in Astrology*, Element Books, 1989.

APPENDIX
The Grades

The use and control of any grade is not *fully implemented* until you have reached the grade above it. So an **Adeptus Minores** (an initiate who has for example developed a contact with the first four spheres of the Tree of Life) will not have full control of those spheres until he/she reaches the stage of **Adeptus Majores**.

These four spheres manifest in the initiate through the powers of Dedication and Self-discipline (Malkuth), control of the astral self and the astral world as it pertains to the initiate and an understanding of the mystery of Yesod.

The next level involves the elements of sacrifice, spiritual agony and endurance that make up the sphere of Tiphereth. At this point the initiate is strong enough to fully cope with and use to advantage the power of the lower four spheres. It is in Tiphereth that one has to face the greatest enemy...oneself. There is an agony of choice between what you know you should do and knowing you could possibly fail if you do not make the right choice. It is the moment when you must give up being part of humanity, for to teach with truth you must stand apart from those you would teach in order to see them clearly. When you make the right choice, the Crown of the Justified is placed upon the head. But that is just the beginning... Then you must walk the path that leads to the **Adeptus Exemptus** grade.

As you approach this grade you begin to understand fully the meaning of what you endured as an Adeptus Majores. The strength that enabled you to 'drink from the cup' comes into its own. You become like the Hermit, standing alone amid the many. There is loss, and sacrifice of the very self as you pass through Geburah. The last flaws of the ego are wrenched from you as you make the long and lonely road towards Chesed. It is this path that will make or break you. This is the path of Exemption and as the initiate progresses he/she comes into their full power. The Sphere of Chesed is the last grade that can be taken in the physical. It is sometimes called the 49th Gate (referring to the 50 Gates of Binah, Binah herself being the 50th). Here in the sphere of Mercy the initiate has one last test.

To offer up all that has been gained, to become as one was in the beginning, to keep nothing but to offer all and wait for what is to come...if it comes. When it does you become exempt... what you become exempt FROM, depends on your own character and any flaws that are left.

There are higher grades, but they are given by a spiritual authority much higher than any human initiate can aspire to while in a physical body. Training in a contacted Mystery School is comparable to entering a Monastery or a Convent. It involves more than the ordinary human being is capable of giving and demands more than most have to give. As in a monastery or convent, there are novices and lay brothers, those who reach a point and find they can go no further in this incarnation...but a start has been made.

All these things show up as possibilities in one's natal chart and are either intensified or show a point of 'this far and no further'. That is what this book is all about, to help you to be aware of what lies before you if you take the road to initiation.

ASTROLOGICAL GLOSSARY

Air (see elements)

Ascendant

The degree or sign of the zodiac rising over the eastern **horizon** at the moment of birth, which marks the **cusp** of the first **house**; hence often referred to as the rising sign. A planet within **orb** of the Ascendant, from either side of the horizon, is also said to be rising. The opposite degree or sign which is simultaneously descending below the western horizon, is called the **Descendant** and marks the cusp of the seventh house.

angular

The term used to describe a planet that falls in one of the houses – first, fourth, seventh and tenth – that define the angles or four cardinal points of a chart, namely, **Ascendant**, **Descendant**, **Midheaven** and **IC**.

aspect

The relationship, measured in degrees of longitude, between two or more planets or other points along the **ecliptic**. The major aspects are the **conjunction** (00°), **sextile** (60°), **square** (90°), **trine** (120°) and **opposition** (180°). The minor aspects are the **quincunx** (also known as the inconjunct) (150°), **sesquiquadrate** (135°), **semi-square** (45°), and **semi-sextile** (30°).

cardinal

The cardinal signs are Aries, Cancer, Libra and Capricorn. They are known for their ability to initiate or to get things going.

Chiron

Discovered in 1977 orbiting between Saturn and Uranus and named after the Centaur in Greek mythology.

conjunction (see aspect)

cusp
The line that marks the division between one house and another in a chart.

direct motion (see retrograde motion)

Earth (see elements)

ecliptic (see *Introduction, Part Two*, page 8)

elements
The four astrological elements are Fire, Earth, Air and Water, which divide the 12 signs of the zodiac into:- Aries, Leo and Sagittarius (the Fire signs); Taurus, Virgo and Capricorn (the Earth signs); Gemini, Libra and Aquarius (the Air signs); and Cancer, Scorpio and Pisces (the Water signs).

Fire (see elements)

fixed
The fixed signs are Taurus, Leo, Scorpio and Aquarius. They are known for their ability to endure.

Grand Cross
A dynamic pattern of energy involving at least four planets in opposition or at right angles to one another.

horizon
The line that runs from the Ascendant to the Descendant in a chart.

house
A chart is divided into 12 houses, each representing a different sphere of life. Going anti-clockwise, the first house starts with the Ascendant and the twelfth ends with it.

IC
IC stands for *imum coeli* (Latin for 'the lowest part of the heavens') and marks the lowest point of a chart; in the Placidus house system (the one used in this book) the fourth house cusp.

inconjunct (see aspect)

intercepted
The term used to describe a sign that is not on a house cusp and hence planets that fall within it. The house with an intercepted sign tends to be larger than one without and so may be of particular importance in the life.

Midheaven

Also called the MC (*medium coeli*, Latin for 'middle of the heavens'), the highest point of a chart; in the Placidus house system, the tenth house cusp.

Moon

The Moon waxes from New, when it is conjunct the Sun, to Full, when it is opposite the Sun and then wanes to New again. This cycle is known as a lunation.

Moon's Nodes (*see Introduction, Part Two*, pages 8-10)

mutable

The mutable signs are Gemini, Virgo, Sagittarius and Pisces. They are known for their ability to adapt.

opposition (see aspect)

orb

The number of degrees allowed for an aspect between planets within which they may be said to exert an influence on each other.

progressed

The term used to describe a planet or other point in the chart based on the technique of secondary progressions or 'day for a year'. This assumes that a day equals a year in the life, with the qualities of the one echoed in the other. Thus the 29th day will correspond to the 29th year and so on.

quincunx (see aspect)

retrograde motion

A planet is said to be retrograde (from the Latin *retrogradi*, 'to go backwards') when it appears to be moving backwards along the zodiacal belt; similarly, it is said to be **direct** when it is moving forwards. When it appears to stand still prior to changing direction, it is said to **station**, or to be stationary.

ruler

The planet that rules a sign. The planet that rules the sign on the Ascendant rules the whole chart.

sextile (see aspect)

square (see aspect)

station (see retrograde motion)

stellium
The term used to describe three or more planets in conjunction or grouped together in one or more signs or houses.

synastry (*see Introduction, Part Two*, page 7)

T-square
A dynamic pattern of energy involving at least three planets, two in opposition and the third at right angles to both.

transit (*see Introduction, Part Two*, page 7)

trine (see aspect)

Water (see elements)

CONTACTS

Esoteric Schools

Servants of the Light
www.servantsofthelight.org

Fraternidad del Círculo Dorado
Plaza del Ángel, L-15 1º Nivel
Guadalajara, Jalisco, México 45000
www.circulo-dorado.org
correo@circulo-dorado.org

The Academy of the Opened Ways
c/o Anubis Training Limited
P.O. Box 9701
Braintree, Essex
CM7 0BG
United Kingdom
www.anubistraining.com
info@anubistraining.com

Astrological Schools

The Centre for Psychological Astrology
BCM Box 1815
London WC1N 3XX
England, UK
Tel/fax +44-20-8749 2330
CPAlondon@dsl.pipex.com
www.cpalondon.com

Faculty of Astrological Studies
BM Box 7470
London WC1N 3XX
England, UK
Tel/fax: +44 (0) 7000 790143
www.astrology.org.uk

ISAR (International Society for Astrological Research)
www.isarastrology.com

NCGR (National Council for Geocosmic Research, Inc)
531 Main St # 1612
New York, NY 10044-0114
USA
(212) 838-NCGR (6247)
www.geocosmic.org

American Federation of Astrologers
6535 S. Rural Rd.
Tempe, AZ 85283-3746
USA
(480) 838-1751
(toll-free) (888) 301-7630
Fax (480) 838-8293
www.astrologers.com

Other Books by The Wessex Astrologer

The Essentials of Vedic Astrology
Lunar Nodes - Crisis and Redemption
Personal Panchanga and the Five
Sources of Light
Komilla Sutton

Astrolocality Astrology
From Here to There
Martin Davis

The Consultation Chart
Introduction to Medical Astrology
Wanda Sellar

The Betz Placidus Table of Houses
Martha Betz

Astrology and Meditation-
The Fearless Contemplation of Change
Greg Bogart

Patterns of the Past
Karmic Connections
Good Vibrations
Soulmates and why to avoid them
Judy Hall

The Book of World Horoscopes
Nicholas Campion

The Moment of Astrology
Geoffrey Cornelius

Life After Grief - An Astrological
Guide to Dealing with Loss
AstroGraphology - The Hidden link
between your Horoscope and your
Handwriting
Darrelyn Gunzburg

The Houses: Temples of the Sky
Deborah Houlding

Through the Looking Glass
The Magic Thread
Richard Idemon

Temperament: Astrology's
Forgotten Key
Dorian Geiseler Greenbaum

Astrology, A Place in Chaos
Star and Planet Combinations
Bernadette Brady

Astrology and the Causes of War
Jamie Macphail

Flirting with the Zodiac
Kim Farnell

The Gods of Change
Howard Sasportas

Astrological Roots:
The Hellenistic Legacy
Joseph Crane

The Art of Forecasting
using Solar Returns
Anthony Louis

Horary Astrology Re-Examined
Barbara Dunn

Living Lilith - Four Dimensions of the
Cosmic Feminine
M. Kelley Hunter

Your Horoscope in Your Hands
Lorna Green

Primary Directions
Martin Gansten

Classical Medical Astrology
Oscar Hofman

Understanding Karmic Complexes:
Evolutionary Astrology and Regression
Therapy
Patricia L. Walsh

www.wessexastrologer.com